POVERTY,
RICHES
AND
WEALTH

"Everything in our lives is interconnected. Yes, this means that even our finances are connected to our faith. Kris Vallotton eloquently explains the ideas of *Poverty, Riches and Wealth* in a way that is inspirational and calls us to action. Your life will be enriched by reading this book."

Banning Liebscher, author, *Rooted: The Hidden Places Where God Develops You*; founder and pastor, Jesus Culture

"Kris has done it again! He's challenged us to rethink what we've grown to believe. This time it's about wealth, riches and poverty. Throughout every day we are making choices that will lead us along pathways to either wealth or poverty. With simple language and challenging insight, *Poverty, Riches and Wealth* is a powerful navigation tool that will help ensure you reach the destiny God has in store for you."

Sandy Stimpson, mayor, Mobile, Alabama

"Kris is a man who speaks the truth. This important book is based on his real life experiences. Kris has helped me go from riches to rags and now back to riches in a new, meaningful life. Read this and deploy it in your life. Watch what happens!"

Michael Clifford, entrepreneur and venture catalyst

"Kris Vallotton has done it again! He has taken one of the most complex and controversial subjects and explained it in practical language. More important yet, he did it with divine anointing that communicates more than concepts; he communicates life. God has gifted Kris with an ability to explain complex issues in a manner that makes them not only understandable but also desirable. Once you pick up this book, you will not want to put it down, and after you have read it, you will find yourself propelled to do higher and better things for God and for society. In *Poverty, Riches and Wealth*, Kris combines unique spiritual insights with engaging humor to present God's will for His children. By showing that the key to prosperity is generosity, Kris delivers believers from the snare of the destructive narcissism created by the 'name it and claim it' doctrine. This is definitely a must-read book."

Dr. Ed Silvoso, author, *Ekklesia: Rediscovering God's Instrument for Global Transformation*; founder and president, Transform Our World Network

"It would be a staggering understatement to suggest that we in the Western Church could use a solidly biblical view of wealth and prosperity. Many of us have longed for this as the deer panteth for the water, and then some. That Kris Vallotton has given us just that in this wonderful, vital book is a cause for genuine thanksgiving."

Eric Metaxas, *New York Times* bestselling author,
*Martin Luther: The Man Who Rediscovered God
and Changed the World* and *Miracles*

"*Poverty, Riches and Wealth* is both foundational and practical in helping you understand true wealth from a Kingdom perspective. Kris Vallotton describes how wealth is an inside job and flows from our beliefs about our identity in Christ and His great love for us. God is waiting to pour out wealth on a people who will use it not to build their own kingdom, but to bring the resources of the Kingdom of God to transform the world around them. As you read this book, ask yourself how you would live if you truly believed that the wealth of heaven was available to do all that is in your heart."

Julie Winter, nurse practitioner; Redding City Council;
author, *ReNew: Breaking Free from Negative
Thinking, Anxiety, and Depression*

"I have had the honor of knowing Kris Vallotton for years. He is a dynamic teacher, a steadfast friend, a revelatory writer and a father to this generation. Kris carries a life-changing message of knowing your identity in Christ and imparts the Father heart of God every time he speaks or writes. I know that the powerful message of Kingdom wealth that Kris lays out in *Poverty, Riches and Wealth* will bring transformation to individuals, communities and even entire nations."

Christine Caine, founder, A21 and Propel

"I've been watching Kris and the Bethel crew for some years now, intrigued by how they nail critical principles that are virtually unknown in the evangelical community. Now Kris has written about poverty, riches and wealth, and in my opinion, it's happened again. I've known a very small number of people who live out Kingdom wealth subconsciously, and everybody admires them. This, however, is the first time I've seen these life-changing principles explained and laid out clearly in print."

Joe Ritchie, founder and chairman, Chicago Research and Trading

"*Poverty, Riches and Wealth* is a very timely work indeed and will encourage many to step out into faith and become key players, helping lead and fund the greatest harvest of souls ever known to man. This harvest has already begun and is underway in many nations around the earth, as you may be aware. Kris has clearly identified the issues of fear, greed, poverty mentality and several others that hold us back from the necessary risk required to change this world at every level. Read this; become a giver, not a taker; and help bring the will of God and the Kingdom of God to earth as it is in heaven."

John Arnott, Catch The Fire, Toronto

"For centuries, the Church has associated piety with poverty, but fortunately, there is a universal principle constantly contradicting this belief—that when poor people are taught to give, their economic circumstances change exponentially. In more than five decades of pastoral ministry, I have seen that it is virtually impossible to remain poor when one faithfully obeys God's laws of Kingdom stewardship. Kris Vallotton's gift is his ability to simplify through precept and example God's desire to prosper His people."

Bishop Joseph L. Garlington Sr., founding pastor,
Covenant Church of Pittsburgh

"*Poverty, Riches and Wealth* introduces a whole new framework for navigating one of my toughest challenges as a business leader—integrating faith, work and finances. Kris recasts wealth and poverty into mindsets, places them both in a spiritual context and then grounds everything with practical advice. He seeks to inject peace and potential where fear and hopelessness often reign. I haven't stopped thinking about this book."

Rob Pace, former partner, Goldman Sachs; founder
and CEO, HundredX

"In Church history, we find two extremes regarding money: One exalted poverty as a virtue, and the other exalted riches. Author Kris Vallotton rises above the muddy rhetoric of much present-day conversation on the subject to draw attention to the reality of the Kingdom of God and its effect on our finances. *Poverty, Riches and Wealth* is practical yet profound. Inspiring in its ability to bring hope to the most broken situation, it taps into God's patterns for an abundant life. Such a blessed life starts on the inside and then affects the external. I pray this book will have lasting impact on how the Church thinks about this very important subject, as it is impossible for us to successfully disciple nations with anything less than an abundance in all things."

Bill Johnson, senior leader, Bethel Church, Redding, California;
author, *God Is Good, The Power That Changes the World* and more

"We serve a covenant-keeping God who has given us a covenant of wealth. We are told to remember that the Lord has given us power to get wealth so that He may confirm the covenant he swore to Abraham as it is this day. This covenant of wealth is for today. Kris Vallotton's book *Poverty, Riches and Wealth* gives us the the tools necessary to unlock the power to get wealth established by God."

Apostles Tony and Cynthia Brazelton,
Victory Christian Ministries International

"When I finished Kris Vallotton's new book, *Poverty, Riches and Wealth*, I had such a rich experience that I felt sad it was over. Not to say it wasn't a complete book on the subject. I feel like I am a relatively healthy person in regard to the concept of the book, but in reading it, I was rewired. Seriously, I couldn't think of one person in my life who doesn't need this book. Kris's wealth of perspective in all its balance and glory will kill wrong thinking and behavior that so permeates the Church today. You'll find yourself in the pages and stories, and at its end you will find yourself, like me, adjusted to thrive."

Shawn Bolz, president, Bolz Ministries

"In John 10:10, Jesus tells us, 'The thief does not come except to steal, and to kill, and to destroy. I have come that they may have life, and that they may have it more abundantly' (NKJV). Jesus has imbued us with abundant life 'to the full,' 'exceeding and surpassing.' This abundance is the kind of Kingdom wealth mentality that *Poverty, Riches and Wealth* seeks to bring to the body of Christ. Kris Vallotton brings a powerful revelation to light: the difference between true Kingdom wealth (which far exceeds simply finances) and merely riches (which settles for money but does not transform an impoverished spirit). Kris imparts an understanding about the wholeness of true wealth, where there is no lack or shortage of health, peace, relationships, finances and more. *Poverty, Riches and Wealth* also exposes the familiarity and elevation of poverty that the Church has historically embraced. Through Kris's own renewal of the mind from a poverty mindset, he shows us that Kingdom wealth is actually about our being able to live out Jesus' own prayer, that God's Kingdom would come on earth and be represented here, as it is in heaven."

Dr. Ché Ahn, president, Harvest International Ministry;
founding pastor, HROCK Church, Pasadena, California;
international chancellor, Wagner University

"What a great book on wealth! This is a scary subject in a lot of circles, yet in reality we need wealth to advance the Kingdom of God. I love truth and I love clarity, and this book has both! Get it, read it and live it!"

Brian Johnson, president, Bethel Music;
songwriter/worship pastor, Bethel Church,
Redding, California

POVERTY, RICHES *and* WEALTH

MOVING FROM A LIFE OF LACK

into

TRUE KINGDOM ABUNDANCE

KRIS VALLOTTON

Chosen

a division of Baker Publishing Group
Minneapolis, Minnesota

© 2018 by Kris Vallotton

Published by Chosen Books
11400 Hampshire Avenue South
Bloomington, Minnesota 55438
www.chosenbooks.com

Chosen Books is a division of
Baker Publishing Group, Grand Rapids, Michigan

Printed in the United States of America

Library of Congress Control Number: 2017961447

ISBN 978-0-8007-9901-4

Unless otherwise indicated, Scripture quotations are from the New American Standard Bible®, copyright © 1960, 1962, 1963, 1968, 1971, 1972, 1973, 1975, 1977, 1995 by The Lockman Foundation. Used by permission. (www.Lockman.org)

Scripture quotations identified MESSAGE are from THE MESSAGE. Copyright © by Eugene H. Peterson 1993, 1994, 1995, 1996, 2000, 2001, 2002. Used by permission of NavPress. All rights reserved. Represented by Tyndale House Publishers, Inc.

Scripture quotations identified NKJV are from the New King James Version®. Copyright © 1982 by Thomas Nelson, Inc. Used by permission. All rights reserved.

Cover design by LOOK Design Studio

Author is represented by The FEDD Agency

18 19 20 21 22 23 24   7 6 5 4 3 2 1

I dedicate this book to all who find themselves struggling to survive, running against the wind and/or imprisoned by life's circumstances. It's my greatest prayer that those who, like me, were born losers would become the world's earthen treasures and God's heavenly hope.

Contents

Foreword

In Christian circles, the topic of poverty and wealth is often met with controversy. Many people wonder how their financial situation matters to God, if at all. Know this: God's dream for you is so much bigger than yours. He promises prosperity and good success. Why is this important? Because it does matter to God. He can take you beyond anything you ever imagined, and He can take you places you have only dreamed about.

I find most people are bound by a spirit of limitation. They believe they will never achieve anything. They believe they will never get past their poverty. They believe God blesses only certain people.

The enemy wants nothing more than to keep God's people chained to a spirit of lack and limitation. God wants the opposite. The key to living a prosperous life—and this doesn't apply solely to finances—is to invest our resources, our time and our gifts into others. We are Kingdom investors. We are blessed to bless others. After all, we can't bring anything with us in the end.

A freeing teacher, my friend Kris explores with wisdom and solid biblical foundation in this book how to gain a perspective on Kingdom wealth. We must be grounded in our identity in Christ. We must understand God's love for us. We must know the difference between riches and wealth—and believe me, there is a difference.

I am so glad I worship the living God who wants me to prosper. He gave all things to us to enjoy in Christ. The difference between living in prosperity and living in poverty is a choice. Choices have consequences. God told Israel that He set life and death, blessing and cursing, before them. They had to choose life or death (see Deuteronomy 30:19).

It is not by chance that you are blessed. It is by choice. It is God's will to give you prosperity with a purpose, to make you a blessing to others. We are not owners of anything; we are stewards of everything He has given us.

I am confident Kris will inspire you through his words. Walk with him through his own story, and learn how his outlook has been shaped over the years. You will be encouraged that God wants more for you than you may think He does.

Jentezen Franklin, senior pastor, Free Chapel, Gainesville, Georgia

Acknowledgments

I want to thank Michael Clifford for teaching me about the power-of-possibility thinking. I am grateful to Joe Ritchie for exposing me to the advantages of unorthodox (out-of-the-box) mindsets. I also want to thank Bill Johnson for demonstrating outrageous generosity to me. And finally, I want to express my deepest gratitude to my wife, Kathy, who has shaped our world through her divine stewardship and selfless courage.

Introduction

Attitudes of Nobility

My father drowned when I was three years old, leaving my mother penniless and with two small children to feed. It was the late 1950s, and the social welfare programs in America provided bare sustenance. We moved into the projects, surrounded by other people who were, for various reasons, stuck in the same system of poverty as we were. I soon learned that there was a kind of camaraderie among poor people, fueled by our strong feelings about our common enemies. We all despised wealthy folks, railed against big business and blamed Uncle Sam for our deprived condition, to name just a few of our targets. We were little, powerless people lost in the sea of humanity, paddling hard but getting nowhere. The winds of financial adversity pounded against our tiny boats, and as if that were not bad enough, wealthy cruise ships passed us in haste, leaving us to contend with their wake. This further reminded us of the inconsiderate ways of the rich and cemented in our minds the stone wall of indifference that divided the "haves" from the "have-nots" of the world.

I was saved at eighteen years old and became part of an amazing church. We were princes in a royal family, or at least that is what I thought. But I soon discovered that God's noble people also despised wealth and actually had the same mentality as the people I grew up with in the projects. Despite the fact that we all yearned for a heavenly Kingdom with gold streets and pearl gates, and that we knew our heavenly Father was rich beyond comprehension, we still gravitated toward poverty like a tick on a dog's behind!

We actually created doctrines to enshrine poverty, as if it were the pinnacle of spiritual enlightenment, the Mount Rushmore of Christianity. We made Jesus poor, forgetting that He was the architect of heaven and Creator of the earth. We viewed His disciples as homeless transients wandering from village to village, spreading the news of sacrifice and piety, and eking out a meager existence from a few coins dropped in the offering by a widow or two.

Paul's exhortation to his beloved Timothy was inscribed in the halls of our conscience, like the thundering voice of God echoing from some holy mountain: "For the love of money is a root of all sorts of evil, and some by longing for it have wandered away from the faith and pierced themselves with many griefs" (1 Timothy 6:10). It is not that we did not know there were "others" (other Scriptures, that is); it is just that we whispered them in dark corners, in secret dialogues with only our most trusted friends. Then, every once in a while, it would happen: A close comrade would break ranks with the righteous and set sail into the treacherous waters of wealth or riches. We would watch as his or her soul was carried out to sea, a tiny boat disappearing on the distant horizon, never to return again.

I got married two years after I was saved, and I carried my poverty prejudice with me into my marriage. Kathy and I worked hard and eventually owned nine businesses, several of which were very successful, but I determined that we would never get lost in the sea of prosperity. We anchored our souls to the shore of sacrifice and stayed there for 22 long years. I also etched these values deep in the hearts of our four kids, instilling in them the noble virtues of sacrifice and piety. I warned them of the dangers of wealth, recounting the stories of those who dared to hoist their anchors and lose sight of the safe shores of poverty and small thinking.

We left the business world and moved out of the mountains to Redding, California, where Kathy and I became pastors at Bethel Church. A few months passed without any significant change in my heart, at least that I was aware of. Then suddenly, it all happened—my poverty spirit crashed on the shores of adversity and my tiny boat of small thinking began to break apart, torn by wave after wave of revelation. The Scriptures that used to be my safety net were now ripping under the weight of exponential increase. I scurried around in a panic, trying desperately to mend my broken nets of poverty, but they simply could not carry the load of prosperity that was being charged to our account.

We were becoming the very ones we had warned people about, and it scared the heck out of me. The "others" (other Scriptures, I mean) that we had uttered in secret with just a few friends, were now being shouted in public from podiums, in classrooms and on our social platforms. It was our coming-out party, but we were not the ones throwing the party. God was! We were being financially blessed to the point that it was becoming ridiculous—even embarrassing—at times.

I really had two primary fears. First, I worried that we would be thought of like the guys who abused the faith message and seemed to measure their spirituality by the stuff they owned. I certainly never measured my spirituality (or anyone else's, for that matter) by what we owned. The truth be known, I had never had enough to be tempted to do that.

Second, I was concerned that people would think we were mismanaging the money they donated to our ministries and were using it for our personal gain. We had lived very modestly our entire life, primarily because there was no other option. There simply had not been enough money to do much more than meet our very basic needs. Then suddenly, thousands of dollars began pouring in from a number of different sources, from real estate deals to book sales, and from teaching materials to conference offerings. Thousands of dollars found their way into our bank accounts. Soon we were giving away about half our profit, yet there was still enough left over to live in abundance. The whole thing came to a climax in May 2016, when a man I had never met before insisted on paying off our house, to the tune of $487,000! (I recount that story for you in chapter 6.)

The payoff of our house was the final straw for me. I saw it as a confirming sign from God, and I was compelled to tell the world what the Lord was revealing to us about wealth. I felt like one of the four lepers who discovered a feast in the midst of a severe famine in the city of Samaria. In the middle of feasting at the banquet table left behind by a fleeing enemy, the lepers said to one another, "We are not doing right. This day is a day of good news, but we are keeping silent" (2 Kings 7:9). I knew I had to brave the criticism of those who would question my motives and/ or methods and write a book about true Kingdom wealth. I think this revelation is a catalyst to overthrowing the principality called Mammon and establishing a wealth mentality rooted in heavenly wisdom. My primary motive in writing this book is to break the back of poverty and release a spirit of prosperity on the world. When I use the word *prosperity*, I don't mean the world's definitions of riches; I mean true Kingdom wealth. Here is a short synopsis of Kingdom wealth:

God's Definitions of Wealth

1. Wealth is the ability (resources, strength and wisdom) to create positive outcomes in the midst of lack, poverty and/or emptiness.

2. Wealth is light in the darkness, healing in sickness, prosperity in poverty, wholeness in brokenness, favor in obscurity, love for the unlovely, beauty for ashes and victors among victims.

3. Wealth is a "can-do" attitude, a "more than enough" mindset and a "nothing is impossible" belief system.

4. Wealth is radical generosity, extraordinary compassion, sacrificial giving and profound humility.

5. Wealth is always thankful and never jealous; it does not brag, it celebrates others and it looks to the future.

My prayer is that you would find keys in this manuscript that would unlock your legacy and release prosperity on your children's children. I hope that you will be so transformed by the revelation in this book that it will literally alter the course of your history. May it be on earth as it is in heaven!

PART ONE

The True Meaning
of Kingdom Wealth

I n the first part of this book, we will discuss the true meaning of
Kingdom wealth as we contrast it with poverty and riches. I will
prove that there is a power to make wealth and that there is a
spirit behind poverty. I will also help you discover how to embrace
the abundant life that Jesus promised and how to avoid becoming
rich instead of wealthy.

1

The Net Worth of Jesus

In July 2016, I was invited to meet Pope Francis with a small group of pastors at the Vatican in Rome. I was rocked by the invitation; not that I had anything I wanted to say or ask of him, but come on . . . how many people in the world get to have a sit-down meeting with the Pope of the Catholic Church? I was excited and a little nervous. The day before I left, I lay awake most of the night, envisioning what it was going to be like meeting the Pope. I wanted to make a good impression on him; after all, I was a Protestant pastor and he was a Catholic pope. We were, by the nature of our religious affiliations, archenemies for five centuries!

I spent most of the next morning packing, but I could not decide what to wear. I tried on all seven of my suits, fifteen dress shirts and twenty-five ties. I finally narrowed my selection down to two, but I could not make up my mind. Should I wear my three-piece gray pinstripe suit with my black silk shirt and black tie, or should I wear my two-piece black suit with my gray silk shirt and red Garcia tie? I tried both suits on several times, changing the combination of shirt, tie and shoes. I finally decided that I would bring them both and resolve the issue when I arrived at the Vatican. Of course, each suit required a different pair of shoes, so I polished all four shoes to make sure I was prepared. I was concerned that the suits would be wrinkled when I arrived at my destination, so I packed my portable steamer in my special fold-over suitcase. I also went out and bought two new pairs of socks, one to match each of my suits. I was so ready!

The next morning I got up at 3:00 a.m., put on some comfortable jeans and my Batman shirt and began my two-day journey to the Vatican. I had four connecting flights and several long layovers before I would reach my final destination. But before I could board my fourth flight, the airline announced that the flight was canceled. *What?!* Suddenly, two hundred people rushed the ticket counter and tried to find alternative flights to get to their destinations. United Airlines finally agreed to put me on another airline—a flight that arrived at the Vatican six hours later. Although I would not be getting much sleep before our meeting with Pope Francis, at least I would get there in time. I was a happy camper.

When I finally arrived in Rome, I was completely exhausted. I dragged my tired hiney down two escalators and arrived at the luggage carousel, along with a couple hundred other exhausted passengers. It was 10:00 p.m. in Rome, and I still had to catch a taxi to the Vatican. The luggage took forever to reach the carousel. Finally, the beautiful sound of the buzzer began to blare. Then another half hour passed, leaving three passengers without luggage, and yes, you guessed it: I was one of them.

"Unbelievable!" I said out loud. I made my way to the Black Hole Room . . . the place where airline employees try to solve the mystery of your lost luggage. (I heard a rumor that these employees train by trying to find unmatched socks that emerge from dryers.) Thirty more minutes passed, and it was now my turn at the counter. A frazzled-looking woman in her late forties greeted me in Italian.

"Do you speak English?" I inquired.

"No," she responded in a thick accent.

Oh great, I thought. She handed me a form to fill out, which had some pictures of luggage at the bottom. The entire form was in Italian, so for the next twenty minutes, with sign language that was very similar to hieroglyphics, she guided me in her *very* broken English through the process of completing the form.

I googled a picture of the Pope and told her I was meeting with him at 1:00 p.m. the next day. "I need my clothes," I kept repeating. "By noon!" I begged.

She gave me a phone number to call and told me to try calling in the morning.

"Unbelievable!" I repeated out loud again. *Before I left home I was so concerned about what suit I should wear, and now I might have to meet the Pope in my crummy Batman shirt and ragged jeans*, I mused. *Yikes!* I arrived at my hotel at 12:30 a.m. and laid my head on my pillow at 1:00 in the morning. I was exhausted, but my mind insisted on playing movies of meeting the Pope. I imagined myself in my old, ragged Batman shirt and tattered jeans, in the midst of pastors dressed in three-piece suits and Pope Francis in his royal robes. *What would the Pope think of my humble attire?* I mused further. *Maybe he would view my unpretentious situation and conclude that a homeless person had somehow slipped into the Vatican.*

The problem was that my then present situation did not actually represent my true economic reality. The fact is, I am not destitute. I own seven expensive suits. Furthermore, I am not homeless. I actually have a big, beautiful house nestled on three acres of oak trees in a gated community. Simply put, I may have looked poor and homeless, but Rome was not my home. Redding, California, is. Measuring my affluence by observing my situation in Rome therefore would have led you to the wrong conclusion about my monetary condition.

Earth Is Not His Home

Jesus arrived in the flesh on this planet through a woman named Mary. Yet it is important to remember that Jesus did not originate in her womb; she was simply the vehicle that carried Him to earth. She was His plane ride to this dimension. His conception was otherworldly . . . or more accurately, heavenly. Interestingly, look at the phrase the apostle Paul used to describe Jesus' earthly entry: "Being found in appearance as a man, He humbled Himself by becoming obedient to the point of death, even death on a cross" (Philippians 2:8). Jesus *found Himself in appearance* as a man—now, that phrase is intriguing in numerous ways! First and foremost, it is essential that we understand that Jesus is not human; He is, in fact, God. I am not sure how He "found Himself" here. Could He possibly have agreed not to remember His true identity when He entered the earth's atmosphere? Did He have to go through the same process of self-discovery as we do to discover His true identity as the Son of God? Some theologians believe that He did, but whatever the case, one thing is for certain: Earth was not His home.

Much like my condition in Rome with my Batman shirt and ragged jeans, if you make the mistake of judging Jesus' net worth by His humble earthly condition, you will misjudge His prosperity and undermine His mission. The apostle Paul put it like this: "For you know the grace of our Lord Jesus Christ, that though He was rich, yet for your sake He became poor, so that you through His poverty might become rich" (2 Corinthians 8:9).

Wait! What did Paul say? Jesus was rich, *but then* He became poor *so* (*the reason He became poor*) we might become rich. That is incredible!

Jesus' home is heaven. Now, I am not sure where heaven is exactly, but the biblical description of it sounds pretty incredible. For instance, the heavenly Jerusalem has streets of pure gold, like transparent glass, with twelve pearl gates. Each of the gates is a single pearl, and the material of the wall is jasper. Furthermore, the entire city is pure gold, like clear glass (see Revelation 21). Jesus left His heavenly home and was born in a manger. It might be obvious, but a manger is a barn where the Israeli shepherds kept their donkeys, sheep and camels. It would have smelled like manure, been infested with flies and been filled with poop. When our Lord's earthly birth is contrasted to His heavenly home, the reality of Jesus' humble state emerges with startling clarity.

I want to point out again that Jesus became poor for a reason. His celestial mission was to make us wealthy. It is the great exchange—beauty for ashes, joy for mourning, hope for the hopeless, healing for sickness, prosperity for poverty. You get the idea: Jesus called it *abundant life*.

The Wickedness of Wealth?

I want us to stop for a moment while I make a few observations about heaven. First of all, if wealth and riches are inherently evil, what are they doing in heaven? Why would God describe heaven so lavishly if wealth were bad, or even bad for you? For example, can you imagine God describing heaven as a place filled with opium fields and heroin factories? No, because drugs speak to us of evil—bad, addictive, destructive substances that ruin people's lives. In other words, we all know that these substances *in themselves* are destructive, so we would never use them to describe a positive condition. On the other hand, wealth cannot be intrinsically evil, or the Bible would not describe heaven as a place full of unimaginable riches. In fact, if heaven is God's goal for us, then wealth must be a piece of our prize!

Our idea of "poor Jesus" is similarly skewed. Although Jesus left heaven, heaven never left Jesus, because Kingdom prosperity always begins from the inside out. You can put Jesus in a manger, but you can't put a manger in Jesus. Wealth, glory and power seeped out of His pores like sweat on a hardworking man on a hot, humid day.

Here is a case in point: Jesus went to a wedding in a village called Cana. Soon after He arrived, the party was in danger of ending prematurely because they did not buy enough wine to sustain all the guests. Mary, His mother, convinced Him to make more wine for the wedding. Jesus ordered the waiters to fill six stone waterpots with water. The water *instantly* turned to wine (see John 2:1–11). There were no grapes necessary, which means the entire process of growing the vines and picking the grapes was bypassed. Furthermore, the long process of fermenting the wine, which takes years to complete, was also circumvented. When the headwaiter tasted the wine, he was stunned because it was so good.

It is important to remember that Mary is the one who insisted that Jesus make wine. How did Mary know that Jesus could make wine from water? Could she have experienced Jesus making wine at home? My point is that if Jesus could make wine from water in two minutes, then it stands to reason that He may have been living modestly on the outside, but wealth flowed out of His innermost being. Mary and Joseph may have been a middle-class carpenter family, but they might have been drinking wine that reminded them of heaven at home. In fact, the wine was so good that the Bible says that when Jesus made wine, He "manifested His glory." Now, that is great wine! I guess He was not kidding when He said that He is the vine and we are the branches (see John 15:1–14).

The Tax Man

One time Jesus and Peter were traveling together without Judas, who carried the money box. When they came to the village of Capernaum, the tax collector insisted that they both pay a poll tax. Although Jesus felt as though they were being taxed unfairly, He instructed Peter to go down to the sea and catch the first fish that bit his hook. Then he was to look in its mouth for a shekel (a coin) and use the money to pay their tax bill (see Matthew 17:24–27).

Did you catch the full impact of what just happened? Jesus just commanded a fish to produce the money they needed to pay their taxes. Did the fish find the money at the bottom of the sea, from some wrecked merchant ship, or did Jesus supernaturally cause a coin to appear in the fish's mouth? I have no idea, but I do know this: If Jesus could command one fish to bring Him money, then He certainly could command a school of fish to duplicate that miracle a thousand times if He needed to. I guess my mama was right; money doesn't grow on trees. But maybe it does grow on seaweed.

Apparently, Jesus took God's command to "rule over the fish of the sea" seriously (Genesis 1:26), because He became quite famous for impacting the fishing industry. The gospels record Jesus supernaturally chumming the fish into the disciple's nets on at least two occasions. Take a look at the first one:

> When He [Jesus] had finished speaking, He said to Simon, "Put out into the deep water and let down your nets for a catch." Simon answered and said, "Master, we worked hard all night and caught nothing, but I will do as You say and let down the nets." When they had done this, they enclosed a great quantity of fish, and their nets began to break; so they signaled to their partners in the other boat for them to come and help them. And they came and filled both of the boats, so that they began to sink.
>
> Luke 5:4–7

These guys are not fishing recreationally; this is how they make their living. Fishing was a middle-class, feast-or-famine kind of occupation . . . that is, until Jesus showed up. He quickly transformed a meager living into a prosperous vocation.

Let's look at one more fishing expedition so we understand that the previous story was not an isolated incident. It was the nature of Jesus to behave extravagantly. He never provided just a few more fish . . . heck no!

> Jesus stood on the beach; yet the disciples did not know that it was Jesus. So Jesus said to them, "Children, you do not have any fish, do you?" They answered Him, "No." And He said to them, "Cast the net on the right-hand side of the boat and you will find a catch." So they cast, and then they were not able to haul it in because of the great number of fish. Therefore that disciple whom Jesus loved said to Peter, "It is the Lord." So when Simon Peter heard that it was the Lord, he put his outer garment on (for he was stripped for work), and threw himself into the sea. But the other disciples came in the little boat, for they were not far from the land, but about one hundred yards away, dragging the net full of fish.
>
> John 21:4–8

Jesus is into the boat-sinking, way-too-many, catch-of-the-year kind of fishing. In America we say time is money, but in the fishing business fish are money. Jesus was not just increasing their catch; He was increasing their cash! It is worth mentioning here that if having a lot of money is a bad thing, then Jesus should have made sure they had minimal catches.

What I am pointing out is that if Jesus can circumvent the process of wealth creation by creating money out of thin air, or by making wine instantaneously from water, or by taking a boy's lunch and multiplying it ten thousand times to feed a crowd that would fill an entire NBA basketball stadium, or by increasing a fisherman's catch by 1,000 percent, then there is *no way* He can ever be called poor . . . at least by worldly standards. Yes, Jesus became poor when you contrast His heavenly home with His earthly visitation. But Jesus was no homeless transient, traversing the countryside with twelve vagabonds. He actually was a famous traveling rabbi who grew up in a middle-class carpenter's home and had a very well-funded ministry.

Funded by the Wealthy

Although Jesus was born in a manger, His birth was announced with astonishing fanfare. God assigned a star to Jesus that the Magi followed to find the Messiah. The Magi were wise men from the East that later tradition holds to be three kings named Casper, Melchior and Balthazar. These kings brought gold, frankincense and myrrh from their treasures and presented them to Jesus at His birth (see Matthew 2:10–11). It seems to me that if you are a king who has been looking into the heavens for years in anticipation of a star that would direct you to the coming Messiah, then the birth of Christ would be a massive event for you. This is not an average birthday where you bring a token gift . . . no way! This is a historic occasion worthy of a substantial gift. In fact, the Bible says it this way: "Opening their treasures, they presented to Him gifts" (verse 11). They did not reach into their moneybags and pull out a few dollars to put into a birthday card; instead, they carried a treasure chest with them because they were presenting Jesus with a large, kingly gift.

Many scholars believe that Jesus had a substantial amount of money from the Magi treasury that launched Him into ministry. Yet traveling for three and a half years with twelve other men had to be pretty expensive. Luke the physician tells us in his gospel how Jesus created financial sustainability in His ministry:

He began going around from one city and village to another, proclaiming and preaching the kingdom of God. The twelve were with Him, and also some women who had been healed of evil spirits and sicknesses: Mary who was called Magdalene, from whom seven demons had gone out, and Joanna the wife of Chuza, Herod's steward, and Susanna, and many others who were contributing to their support out of their private means.

Luke 8:1–3

Jesus had several wealthy friends who helped support His needs and the expenses of His ministry team. Many of His biggest supporters were wealthy women. The life of Mary and Martha, Lazarus's sisters, demonstrates the level of affluence many of Jesus' friends had. Mary poured a vial of perfume—pure nard, in fact—over Jesus' feet and wiped them with her hair. That single vial was worth as much as a year's wages! Think about it; if you can afford perfume worth an average person's annual salary, it just stands to reason that you are quite wealthy (see John 12:1–9). Although Jesus did spend a lot of time with the poor and the broken, He could also be found hanging out a lot with Mary, Martha and Lazarus. They were His best friends and probably His primary financial supporters.

Fox Holes and Bird Nests

Much of the misunderstanding about the status of Jesus' personal financial condition comes from a story told in the gospels of both Matthew and Luke. Jesus was walking down a road with His disciples when a guy yelled out, "I will follow You wherever You go!" (Luke 9:57).

In typical Jesus fashion, He responded, "The foxes have holes and the birds of the air have nests, but the Son of Man has nowhere to lay His head" (verse 58). Then Jesus turned to another man and said, "Follow Me."

The guy wanted to follow Jesus, but he had a practical reason why he could not leave right away. He replied, "Lord, permit me first to go and bury my father" (verse 59).

Jesus seemed a little miffed at the guy's response. He demanded, "Allow the dead to bury their own dead; but as for you, go and proclaim everywhere the kingdom of God" (verse 60).

Some people are convinced that Jesus was telling the first guy that He was homeless and that following Him meant camping out on the ground. This seems like a rational assumption, until we investigate a little further. Consider the story of the Last Supper. Jesus needed a place that would seat thirteen men, not to mention someone to prepare a Passover meal for all of them. By the way, preparing a kosher Passover meal for a group that size is no small feat. Yet Jesus had it all handled:

> His disciples said to Him, "Where do You want us to go and prepare for You to eat the Passover?" And He sent two of His disciples and said to them, "Go into the city, and a man will meet you carrying a pitcher of water; follow him; and wherever he enters, say to the owner of the house, 'The Teacher says, "Where is My guest room in which I may eat the Passover with My disciples?"' And he himself will show you a large upper room furnished and ready; prepare for us there." The disciples went out and came to the city, and found it just as He had told them; and they prepared the Passover.
>
> Mark 14:12–16

We can deduce from this story (and many others) that the people who were supporting Jesus' ministry took really good care of Him. It is therefore unlikely that Jesus would have had any problem finding housing for His disciples when they traveled. It is more likely that His "foxes have holes and birds have nests" comment had more to do with the heart of the person who was inquiring than it did with the accommodations available in that location. Especially since a few seconds later, Jesus turned to another guy and said, "Follow Me." If Jesus were telling the first guy, "I'm sorry you can't go with us; I have no accommodations for you," then why did He invite the other guy to travel with Him? Again, Jesus was not homeless.

Traveling Light

When Jesus sent His disciples out alone on missionary journeys, He did require them to travel light. He told them, "Do not acquire gold, or silver, or copper for your money belts, or a bag for your journey, or even two coats, or sandals, or a staff; for the worker is worthy of his support" (Matthew 10:9–10). His reasoning was that He wanted the local people to house and care for the disciples. He considered their labor (preaching the Gospel, healing the sick and casting out demons) worth paying for.

Jesus went on to say, "Whatever city or village you enter, inquire who is worthy in it, and stay at his house until you leave that city" (verse 11). This is a brilliant strategy in that noble people were required to invest in their own spiritual growth by caring for the practical needs of those who were ministering to them.

Not only were the disciples able to cover ground more quickly with this arrangement, but also the local people were much more likely to value something they had to sacrifice for. Furthermore, the disciples were commissioned to release a supernatural peace on every home they lodged in, so the local townspeople were able to experience the same peace that was on the disciples' lives (see verses 12–13).

Dressed for Success

Not only was Jesus not homeless; He actually dressed well for His day. If you compared Jesus' clothes to the people of that time, you would have to conclude that He was at least somewhat affluent. Jesus wore a seamless tunic woven in one piece. When He was crucified, the four soldiers who stripped Him cut His outer garments into four pieces so that they each got something. But because His tunic was seamless, it was so valuable that the soldiers gambled for it (see John 19:23–25). Some modern theologians call His seamless tunic the Armani suit of the first century.

Let me be clear: I am not trying to propose that Jesus was a rich tycoon on earth, although He clearly had the means to be one through the supernatural abilities He demonstrated. What I am trying to point out is that Jesus was not poor by any earthly standard. He had everything He needed to take care of His team and cover their travels. He was incredibly generous, He often helped people prosper financially, and He taught more parables about money than about any other subject.

Jesus was very aware that the way people handled money was often a reflection of what was going on in their hearts. For instance, He complimented a widow who gave her last cent in an offering, and He rebuked a young ruler who cared more about riches than he did about his soul. He taught people to invest money rather than bury it, and He explained to us that we have to be faithful with unrighteous wealth before God will give us true riches. We will investigate these subjects further in the chapters ahead, but it should suffice to say here that Jesus was no pauper.

Well, for those of you who are curious about the rest of the story of my trip to Rome: My luggage arrived three hours before our meeting with the Pope; thus, my reputation was preserved. By the way, I went with the brown two-piece suit with the black shirt and brown striped silk tie. (I packed the brown suit at the last minute in the middle of the night, and it's a good thing I did.)

2

How to Cure
a Wealth Autoimmune Disease

Kathy and I sold our four businesses and moved to Redding, California, in December 1996 to start the Bethel School of Supernatural Ministry. The sale of our auto parts stores was supposed to have provided us with about $250,000 in profit for our twenty years of hard work. Big A Auto Parts, a half-billion-dollar, publicly traded corporation, signed a contract to purchase our auto parts stores in mid-1994. But they somehow managed to drag out our escrow for eighteen months, while reassuring us every week that our escrow would "close next week." So we moved to Redding with their reassurance that the escrow would close very shortly.

A month after we arrived at Bethel Church, Big A Corporation went bankrupt. Consequently, not only did we *not* have a quarter of a million dollars to live on while we were building the school, but we also suddenly owed 1.4 million dollars! Kathy and I had agreed to volunteer until the school start-up could afford to pay us, and now we had no income to pay any of our personal bills or even feed our family. Overnight, we lost everything—our businesses, the house our kids grew up in and almost all of our worldly possessions.

The next week, I met with Bill Johnson and the Bethel Church elders to explain our situation and let them know we were leaving. I told them we were going to have to go bankrupt and find jobs so we could try to pay back as much of our debt as possible. When I finished my long, detailed explanation of our plight, one of the elders stood up and said, "We're a family, and families stay together in tough times. So we don't want you to leave! Furthermore, we believe God can do the impossible, so I want to ask you not to file for bankruptcy for six months, while we pray for a financial miracle for you guys."

"I have no faith for that," I replied honestly.

"Will you trust our faith for six months?" he said confidently.

I thought to myself, *What do I have to lose?* So I agreed to wait six months, as the elders were requesting. But I honestly had no idea what was about to happen next, nor was I prepared for the war that was going to take place inside me as a result.

The following month, we were miraculously forgiven over $900,000 of our debt. A few months later, the Small Business Administration agreed to reduce our $247,000 loan to $11,000 in cash, provided we could pay them in thirty days. The day before the thirty days were up, a man we did not know, directed by God in a dream, gave us a $30,000 check. (You just cannot make this stuff up!) We were able to pay off the SBA and several other bills as well. Within the next three years, all our debt was paid off or forgiven.

Wonderful, right? Sort of, except it unearthed a problem so deep in me that I had no idea it was even there. Many people, like the man I described above, were handing us money left and right. I took their money because I was so desperate, but I was also ashamed of myself. The idea that people would help us simply because they loved us, without any thought of getting anything in return, drove me to a crisis of soul. I avoided everyone who gave to us like the plague, not understanding why, until one special night that I will never forget for the rest of my life. In fact, that night had such a dynamic impact on my life that I have told the story in some of my previous books. I won't retell the whole thing here, but the short version is that after I had been going to great lengths to avoid this man who had given me such a generous gift, God spoke to me and told me that the reason I kept avoiding people who gave to us was that I did not feel worthy of their love or their generosity. Throughout that night, He revealed layer after layer of self-hatred and low self-worth that had plagued me since I was a little boy. Then He said, *It's time for you to love yourself the way I love you!*

I was stunned. We had owned nine businesses over the previous twenty years, and that night I was suddenly aware that I had a poverty mentality that was inoculating me from wealth. Although our businesses almost always performed excellently, my low self-esteem sabotaged our prosperity. Every time we would begin to prosper, I would find some way to siphon off our wealth into some worthless venture.

The great apostle John addressed this dynamic in prayer with those he pastored. He wrote, "Beloved, I pray that in all respects you may prosper and be in good health, just as your soul prospers" (3 John 2). John concluded that the foundation of all prosperity and health is relegated to our soul's prosperity. In other words, our soul's prosperity determines the level of wealth and health that we experience.

This reminds me of a saying that I heard a long time ago that goes something like this: "If you need money, don't ask for money; ask why you need money." I never understood this adage until I had that experience with the man who had given me the large sum of money. As time passed, I came to understand that if you put people in an environment around them that they perceive to be better than the environment within them, then they will reduce the environment around them to match the environment they believe they have within them.

Fatal Detraction

When we live in poverty of soul, our perceived unworthiness, rooted in our lack of self-love, is kind of like turning two magnets in the repelling direction. Although the repelling force is invisible, it is nonetheless a powerful and viable deterrent to any connection. Unworthiness and lack of self-love are an invisible force field, and like those magnets, they repel prosperity and hold us in poverty. In fact, the only way for this magnetic *detraction* to be neutralized is for a stronger outside influence to overcome its resistance.

For example, sometimes a person's skill set is greater than the level of negative magnetic influence that lurks within, which will result in seasons of external prosperity. But that kind of prosperity is never sustainable, because it is impossible to overcome consistently with our talent what our negative identity or mindset is rejecting.

This scenario inside us eventually becomes something like a wealth autoimmune disease. An autoimmune disease occurs when the body's white blood cells, which are assigned to fight off illness, somehow receive the wrong message. Then they rebel against their mission and attack the body itself. When we struggle with self-love, that wealth autoimmune disease kicks in and we feel guilty for our prosperity, so we try to soothe our souls with some kind of penance. At best, this is self-sabotaging; at worst, it is self-destructive.

In a similar way to healthy white blood cells, however, a wealth mindset—a mindset in which we view ourselves as sons and daughters of God—protects us from self-pity, depression and a victim mentality.

Horsepower

Not long ago, I had an experience that reminded me again of this autoimmune dynamic in my own life. On July 19, 2015, Kathy and I celebrated our fortieth anniversary. Kathy wanted to celebrate at Disneyland, the place we went for our honeymoon forty years earlier. Standing in line for hours to take a two-minute ride is not my idea of romance, yet I really wanted to do something special for Kathy, so I joyfully concurred. A few weeks later, we arrived in the land of Disney.

The next day, we were standing in line "enjoying" the rides when Kathy told me that she wanted to buy something special for me for our anniversary and she was wondering what I wanted. I was ready. I shouted, "A yellow Corvette Stingray!"

I knew Kathy was not super excited about me driving a fast car, especially a bright yellow sports car. She stared in my eyes for a long time and then proclaimed, "If that's what you really want, then I want you to have it!"

A month later, a bright yellow 2014 Corvette pulled up in our driveway. It was almost new, stunningly beautiful and incredibly fast. I was beside myself for days. I had grown up around cars and had always loved Corvettes. In my teen years, I built four Corvette models. Moreover, my grandfather owned the first service station in Mountain View, California, and I followed in his footsteps, owning four automotive repair shops and three auto parts stores. So I guess you could say that cars are kind of in my blood!

I really loved my Corvette, but I decided not to drive it to work. (I am a pastor at Bethel Church.) My staff kept asking me when I was going to bring my car to work so they could see it, but I kept avoiding answering the question. A week passed before I finally decided to think through my dilemma. *What, exactly, is my problem?* I asked myself. I decided that the best way to discover what was troubling me was to drive my Vette to work and see what fears forced their way to the surface.

When I arrived at work, several staff members rushed out to see my car. They kept walking around the car, *ooh*ing and *ahh*ing and asking questions.

"How fast does it go?"

"How much horsepower does it have?"

"What year is it?"

Yet I found myself answering questions nobody was asking. "It's used," I said sheepishly. "We got a great deal on it. Kathy bought it for me. Pastor Joe's Escalade cost more," I declared.

A few minutes later, back in my office, I was regretting buying the car. *People are going to think I'm a show-off,* I mused. *A pastor has no business owning a beautiful car like this. What are people going to say about me?* The questions plagued me.

An hour later, my good friend Dann Farrelly came into my office. "Beautiful car, dude," he said with a grin.

"Yeah, I feel sort of bad for buying it," I responded.

"What! Why?" he shot back. "Dude, you're a car guy—this is a perfect car for you. You deserve it, and you have the money for it. Dude, enjoy your car!" he insisted.

"What are people going to think?" I pressed.

"If they can't rejoice with you, then it's their problem! Don't worry about it," he said confidently.

From that day on, I drove my Corvette to work every day. Most people loved it and told me how much they liked the fact that the car guy had finally gotten his dream car. I decided to face down my fears by posting a picture of the Vette on social networking and thanking Kathy publicly for the car. The results were surprisingly positive, with a few exceptions. There is an accuser in every crowd, of course, especially on Facebook. But hundreds of people posted really encouraging comments.

The moral of the story is that it is okay to have nice things, as long as those things don't have you. *Sometimes*, having wonderful things is a sign of something beautiful going on in the heart of a person who is forging his or her way out of a poverty mentality.

Trouble in Paradise

Jesus said, "You shall love your neighbor *as* yourself" (Matthew 19:19, emphasis added). It is surprising how much of an impact those two little letters, *a-s*, can have on a person's life. Your neighbors, co-workers, family members and friends are all being dramatically affected by this two-letter word. In fact, I propose that this tiny word is in charge of your finances, rules your emotional state and dictates how you relate to God.

"*What?*" you protest. "That's ridiculous!"

Let me explain my thesis. The word *as* means "the same." In other words, love your neighbor the same way (or to the same level) *as* you love yourself. Since love looks like something, your behavior toward your neighbor is a reflection of how you feel about yourself. Another way to say it is that the best thing you can do for the people around you is to love yourself.

The great apostle Paul echoes these sentiments when he says, "Husbands ought to love their own wives *as* their own bodies. He who loves his own wife loves himself; for no one ever hated his own flesh, but nourishes and cherishes it, just as Christ also does the church" (Ephesians 5:28–29, emphasis added). There is that tiny word *as* again, but this time instead of helping a neighbor, it is saving a marriage. This two-letter word *demands* an answer to a profound question: *How do you feel about you?*

You may have been taught that humility requires you to feel bad about yourself, or at least not to feel good about who you are. Nothing could be further from the truth. Humility does not dictate how you feel about yourself, but it does determine how you express your self-love to those around you. It is *humility* that requires the love you have for yourself to benefit those around you. For example, when people are telling a story about something they have accomplished and you have a better story, it is *humility* that whispers, *Let them have the best story of the day; give them the spotlight.* It is self-love that makes it easy to give others the stage because your soul is not starving for affection or clamoring for attention. Extending God's love to ourselves first lays a foundation for us to radically love those around us. On the other hand, when we starve our souls of love, we have no source to draw from to truly love others.

True humility is actually derailed by self-hatred and undermined by low self-esteem. This is because humility is not thinking less of yourself; it is just thinking of yourself less. On the other hand, all self-demeaning thoughts center your attention on your sense of *lack*, drawing away your affection for God and others.

Humility means you are teachable, influenceable, correctable and vulnerable. Humility can learn from the least, is moved by a child, embraces a rebuke and lives in authenticity. Humility lets others take a bow while you take a seat. It is honor in action and love authenticated. True humility means that you recognize your need without condemning your soul. Prayer is therefore humility expressed toward God, while thankfulness is humility expressed in gratitude.

Get a Grip

Hopefully, by now you are convinced that loving yourself is the key to a prosperous soul, which is the foundation for becoming wealthy and healthy in every area of your life. The questions that press against your soul in getting there involve the *how* and *what*. Or more specifically, *How do I learn to love myself?* And, *What is the process out of this prison of poverty?* Here are eight simple but profound steps to walking out of poverty and into a prosperous soul.

1. Discover who God says you are.

There are hundreds of Scriptures that reveal your amazing identity in Jesus. I will walk you through a few of them to give you a head start on your journey out of pauperville and into His palace.

The apostle Paul said, "While we were yet sinners, Christ died for us" (Romans 5:8). The connotation is that you used to be a "sinner," someone whose nature it was to sin and do evil. Sin was not just something you did; it was actually your identity. *But* when you received Jesus into your life, you were born again (see John 3:4–8). You became a *saint*, meaning a "holy believer." It is no longer your nature to sin, because you are a holy person and a citizen of a holy nation (see 1 Peter 2:9).

Furthermore, when you asked Jesus into your life, you became a son or daughter of God Himself. So now you are encouraged to call your heavenly Father "Daddy."

Wait, because it gets even better! You are seated on a throne next to Jesus, and you were created to reign with Him throughout eternity because you are His Bride (see Romans 8:14–23; Ephesians 5:25–32; Revelation 21:2–9). (The Bride part is a little hard for us guys to wrap our brains around, but I guess if the ladies can be sons of God, certainly we men can figure out how to be the Bride of Christ.)

The apostle Paul gave us one of my favorite revelations of our identity in Jesus: "Therefore if anyone is in Christ, he is a *new* creature; the old things passed away; behold, *new* things have come"

(2 Corinthians 5:17, emphasis added). The Greek word *new* in this passage means "prototype," or something never before created. You are a prototype creature molded by your Father, modeled after Jesus Christ, infused with miracle power, and filled with wisdom from the age to come. It is really hard to feel bad about yourself when you are a forerunning prototype, never-before-graced-this-planet child of the King!

I want to inspire you to journey through the Scriptures and unearth the full revelation of the mystery of your identity in God. He is waiting eagerly for you to encounter His indescribable, outrageous love for you, so that He might awaken the new you to your fantastic future.

2. Envision yourself as God sees you.

I have discovered a principle in the Kingdom that simply says, "If I can envision it, I can have it." That is not to say that we can selfishly name and claim anything we want, so stay with me. The author of the book of Hebrews puts it like this: "By faith we understand that the worlds were prepared by the word of God, so that what is seen was not made out of things which are visible" (Hebrews 11:3). In other words, everything that God created in the visible realm is a manifestation of His imagination. The book of Genesis says that God made us in His own image and likeness (see Genesis 1:27). What God imagined, we became, and apparently He was imagining Himself, because we were made in His likeness.

The wisest king in the world, Solomon, articulated it like this: "As he [a man] thinks in his heart, so is he" (Proverbs 23:7 NKJV). There is something very powerful about your imagination, which many people from the dark side have perverted, causing most believers rarely to tap into it (at least on purpose). Yet it is vision that shapes our lives and directs our destinies. What you imagine has a huge effect on who you are becoming. You are forming your outer world with your inner thoughts.

When Moses died, his protégé, Joshua, took on the nearly impossible task of leading the children of Israel out of the wilderness in which they wandered for forty miserable years, and into the Promised Land. After decades of determination and anguish, Moses had failed in his divine mission, leaving the task to his willing, but fearful general. God met with Joshua immediately after the death of his faithful leader and gave him some simple but profound insights into how to apprehend his divine destiny successfully. The message was direct, but encouraging; three times in five minutes God exhorted Joshua to be "strong and courageous" and not to be afraid (see Joshua 1:6–9).

It is darned hard not to be afraid when you are tasked with getting 1.5 million civilians into their Promised Land, which is inhabited by enemies and infested with giants, not to mention the fact that the Israelites had no solution for how to cross the Jordan River. Yet in the midst of God's dialogue with Josh, He gave him incredible insight. God said that if Joshua did three simple things, then he would make his own way "prosperous" (there is that word *prosperous* again) and he would "have success." Joshua 1:8 tells us what those three things were:

#1 "This book of the law shall not depart from your mouth."
#2 "You shall meditate on it day and night."
#3 "Be careful to do according to all that is written in it."

These three simple steps have the power to radically alter the course of your life forever. Let's make them practical for you. First of all, get your face into the Book (the Bible) and find out what God says about you and yours. Second, train your tongue to talk as though you believe what God says more than you believe what you see, feel or fear. Third, meditate on the stuff you were reading when you had your face in the Book.

The word *meditate* means to imagine, think about, envision, talk to yourself and even sing the truth to yourself. (If your singing is really bad, I suggest humming, as there is no sense in singing yourself into a tizzy.) Next, take action. What things did you meditate on that require action? Get busy creating action points for all of your identity insights, and soon you will have a wealth mentality.

3. Recount the sins and failures troubling you, and ask forgiveness.

Let me be clear that I am not talking about staring at your belly button or spending your days in regret; I am merely saying that *if* you are still plagued by any past failure(s) or sin(s), then deal with them head on. You need to recount your past sins and failures that still trouble you and ask Jesus to forgive you.

You cannot conquer what you refuse to confront, and buried shame is more dominant than unapplied redemption. Yet closure is so easy in Jesus that it is almost embarrassing! The apostle John said it best: "If we confess our sins, He is faithful and righteous to forgive us our sins and to cleanse us from all unrighteousness" (1 John 1:9). There it is, short and sweet: Confess your sins and He does the rest.

God does not forgive excuses; He only forgives sins. Some people never live in peace because they are too arrogant, stubborn, afraid, etc., to admit that they screwed up . . . it was their fault . . . they got it wrong. So many people ask God for mercy but refuse to admit that they failed. Yet mercy means you did not get what you deserved (punishment). In order to receive mercy, you have to have done something wrong and confess it; otherwise, mercy goes unapplied. When you confess your sins, God forgives them and cleanses you from all unrighteousness.

God actually is able to fix your root issues, cleanse you from impure motives, and release you from *all* addictions. He has power over anything that would imprison you, punish you or reduce you. How do you unleash all heaven's power in your life? Confess your sins and repent. To repent means to view your sins from God's perspective and therefore think about sin the way He does.

4. Ask Jesus to show you your sins or failures from His perspective.

Let's look at a beautiful picture of this in the book of Zechariah:

> Then he showed me Joshua the high priest standing before the angel of the LORD, and Satan standing at his right hand to accuse him. The LORD said to Satan, "The LORD rebuke you, Satan! Indeed, the LORD who has chosen Jerusalem rebuke you! Is this not a brand plucked from the fire?" Now Joshua was clothed with filthy garments and standing before the angel. He spoke and said to those who were standing before him, saying, "Remove the filthy garments from him." Again he said to him, "See, I have taken your iniquity away from you and will clothe you with festal robes." Then I said, "Let them put a clean turban on his head." So they put a clean turban on his head and clothed him with garments, while the angel of the LORD was standing by.
>
> And the angel of the LORD admonished Joshua, saying, "Thus says the LORD of hosts, 'If you will walk in My ways and if you will perform My service, then you will also govern My house and also have charge of My courts, and I will grant you free access among these who are standing here.'"
>
> Zechariah 3:1–7

I love this graphic depiction of Joshua the high priest (a different Joshua than Moses' successor), because it is such a profound picture of the full spectrum of the process of forgiveness. There is Joshua, the guilty soul, who (like all of us) has messed up his life in one way or another. Then there is Satan, who is like a pesky fly that just will not go away, accusing us day and night. Of course, there is also the Lord, our Savior, Friend and Redeemer, who is vicious in His dealings with the devil. He rebukes the danged devil and immediately commands the angels to help us take off our filthy rags of a life and clothe ourselves in His robes of righteousness.

It is so important, especially when you fail, that you see yourself from God's merciful perspective. Envisioning your failure through the eyes of Jesus is essential to assigning the right roles to the proper characters in your life. There is a loud voice shouting, *Guilty! Away to the gallows with this one! Off with his [or her] head!* But it is not the Lord convicting you; it is Satan trying to mess with your head. Satan's goal is to get your eyes off the Lord's redemption and on your own failures. But in the midst of all the shouting and hoopla, there is always the reassuring voice of your Shepherd, reminding you of His amazing power to liberate you from your failures and the devil's plan for your demise. Stay in that quiet place of seeking to see things from Jesus' perspective, until you can see your failings transformed into His fantastic future for you.

5. Ask Jesus about cleanup and closure; then take action.

If Jesus shows you that there are actions you need to take to clean up your mess (or messes) and/or to bring closure to your life, then take action and take care of it. The Bible says that we need to bear the fruit of our repentance (see Matthew 3:8; Acts 26:20). Most of the time, this simply means asking people whom we have wronged to forgive us, and doing what we can to right our wrongs. It is important to note here that you are responsible to do your part, but that you cannot make someone forgive you. Nor is it your job to convince people to exonerate you. Let the Holy Spirit do His part in convincing the other people who are involved to reciprocate your response.

It is also important that you don't do penance, which looks as if you are working for forgiveness or are allowing yourself to be punished for your failures. Jesus forgave you and released you from punishment. Period. Case closed. You are free. Whenever you punish yourself or allow others to punish you for the wrong you did, you are insulting Jesus. You are saying to God through the sign language of your life that what Jesus did on the cross was not good enough for you. Just do your part, and then let God use His *all-powerfulness* to do His part supernaturally.

6. Develop a vetting system for yourself—a truth wall.

It is important to develop a vetting system, or a truth wall, for what you allow yourself to listen to and think about. This is a huge part of a wealth mentality. Jesus gave us profound insights into how our vetting process affects our lives when He said, "Take care what you listen to. By your standard of measure it will be measured to you; and more will be given to you besides" (Mark 4:24).

I pondered this verse for years, asking myself what it means, especially the "more besides" part. In the middle of a marketing class I got my answer. It was 2016, and my team and I were at a workshop on Internet marketing, taught by a world-class instructor. (Anytime we go to a class like this, nobody wants to sit next to me because I am such a tech klutz. Somehow, I always manage to embarrass my team by asking the stupidest questions.) This instructor was explaining how Internet algorithms function (automated reasoning), and how we could use this technology to spread the message of the Kingdom. He showed us how the Internet allows everyone's activity on the Net to be tracked and recorded for life. He explained that there are programs that analyze this statistical data to determine people's interests, desires and passions. This software facilitates target marketing to specific people groups by vetting people's desires, so anyone who has something to sell can present it to people who have a proven interest in that product or service.

In other words, what you watch and listen to creates "desire paths" (called algorithms) that are used to encourage you to buy things from organizations that specialize in a specific product or service. For example, if you do something wrong like look at porn on the Internet, porn sites will determine through algorithms (automated reasoning) what you watch and will send you *more* of the same via ads and porn pictures.

As the instructor was explaining this for like the fifth time (as I said, I am a little slow at this sort of thing), it suddenly hit me like a ton of bricks, and I shouted, "There are algorithms in the spirit! Now I understand the verse that has eluded me for twenty years!"

Of course, nobody there had any idea what I was talking about at the time, but think about it: The things you like listening to invite more of the same in the spirit. *"Take care what you listen to"* because *"by your standard of measure it will be measured to you."* In other words, like the Internet, you determine what you pay attention to. Then by your standard—according to your own desires—it will be measured to you, as the people around you give you what you have an appetite for. But *"more will be given to you besides."* You will also have things presented to you that you did not ask for or even seek after, much like the pop-up ads on your computer screen.

The spirit realm operates much like the Internet. When you choose to entertain certain kinds of thoughts—maybe for you it is worry and fear—you will invite other worriers and fearful people into your world. It is true what they say, that "birds of a feather flock together." And other people whom you have no connection to and no desire to know will mysteriously find you.

On the other hand, if you "watch over your heart [mind] with all diligence" (Proverbs 4:23) and vet your thoughts through God's divine filter, then you will attract like-minded people to you. Furthermore, this principle works in the unseen realm, in that your thoughts attract or resist different kinds of spiritual influences in your life. I like to put it this way: Angels and demons travel at the speed of thought.

7. Make and memorize a list of the five most profound things Jesus says about you.

The goal of this exercise is to help you develop new, positive ways of thinking that will assist you in beginning a powerful and peaceful life that originates with the Kingdom within you. When you proactively spend time pondering the things Jesus says about you, you create new neural pathways in your brain. Neural pathways are the roads in your brain that thoughts travel on. I once heard a neural scientist describe the creation of neural pathways by comparing the process to dropping a hot steel ball bearing into a pound of cheese. The ball bearing represents a thought, and the cheese represents your brain.

Simply stated, whenever you think about a subject, it forges a pathway in your brain, making it easier for you to think about that same subject again (kind of like the path you would create in the physical by walking through a wheat field). The more you entertain the same thoughts, the wider that road becomes in your mind. If you think positive, healthy thoughts a couple of times a week, but spend most of your time thinking about negative, hopeless, destructive thoughts, then metaphorically speaking, you will build a six-lane freeway to a prison camp, while barely hewing out a walking trail to your divine destiny!

The neural pathways you create become mindsets that tend to dictate how you think and what you visualize most easily. Of course, the science of neural pathways is much more complex than this childlike explanation, but it helps to consider a simple illustration to understand how you can proactively affect your outlook on life.

You may have grown up in a family who feasted at the pig trough of ungodly thinking, but you have the power to change all that. It is important to understand that whatever you cultivate in your mind will dominate it. When you remember what Jesus thinks about you and meditate on the profound attributes He shows you about yourself, you are proactively building new roads in your mind, and ultimately, you are altering your destiny. The apostle Paul gave us great insight into this subject when he admonished the Roman believers, "Do not be conformed to this world, but be transformed by the renewing of your mind" (Romans 12:2). The truth is, you cannot change your life, *but* if you change your thoughts, Jesus will transform your life.

8. Ask *how your attributes should affect your actions, and do accordingly, no matter how you feel.*

Ask yourself how someone who has the five attributes that Jesus said you have (the list you just memorized) should think, talk, behave and dream. Then do accordingly, no matter how you feel. Nothing is quite so affirming and confidence building as acting out your God thoughts instead of your feelings.

Your feelings, although important, are great servants, but terrible masters! I am reminded of God's counsel to Cain when jealousy was plaguing the guy:

The LORD said to Cain, "Why are you angry? And why has your countenance fallen? If you do well, will not your countenance be lifted up? And if you do not do well, sin is crouching at the door; and its desire is for you, but you must master it."

Genesis 4:5–7

Did you notice how doing well (or not doing well) was directly related to Cain's countenance (i.e., his attitude)? When you act on the things that Jesus says about you, you forge the truth into your heart and accelerate the transformation process in your mind.

If you have spent your life with a poverty mentality, then thinking and acting differently may not feel real or authentic at first, but persevere, because thirty days from now, there will be a new you. Let me close this chapter by reminding you that you were born to win, and that Jesus is in your corner. If God is for you, then who can be against you?

3

Why All Believers
Should Be Wealthy, Not Rich

The idea that all believers should be wealthy seems offensive, arrogant and prideful at best, and ignorant, exaggerated and misleading at worst. Yet it is 100 percent true all the time. Now, before you decide to jump off my ship and swim to the safety of "Familiar Island," let me be clear that not every believer should be rich, because *rich* and *wealthy* are two completely different things. Let me contrast poverty, riches and wealth for you and see if you agree with me.

I have found that one of the easiest ways to explain an otherwise difficult subject is by contrasting two opposing ideas with one another. It is amazing how viewing things in contrasting descriptions can clarify and quantify truth. In fact, in the book of Proverbs the wisest king who ever lived often used contrasting truths held in tension to reveal his ageless wisdom. Here are a few examples from Solomon's writings:

Ill-gotten gains do not profit, but righteousness delivers from death.

Proverbs 10:2

He who gathers in summer is a son who acts wisely, but he who sleeps in the harvest is a son who acts shamefully.

Proverbs 10:5

The wise of heart will receive commands, but a babbling fool will be ruined.

Proverbs 10:8

Hatred stirs up strife, but love covers all transgressions.

Proverbs 10:12

Now let me demonstrate the difference between people who engage in "wealth thinking" and people who focus on "poverty thinking" by contrasting these two perspectives with one another. It will be easy to grasp these rather complex concepts through these simple illustrations:

1. Poverty lives for today, but wealth leaves a legacy.
2. Poverty finds a problem in every opportunity, while wealth finds an opportunity in every problem.
3. Poverty feels entitled, while wealth feels empowered.
4. Poverty fears the future, yet wealth makes history.
5. Poverty blames others for its condition, but wealth takes responsibility for things that are not its fault.
6. Poverty asks, "What are you going to do for me?" Wealth asks, "Who is worthy of my investment?"
7. Poverty hangs around with other disgruntled sorts who validate its accusations, but wealth surrounds itself with other powerful influencers.

8. Poverty votes for candidates who will increase its entitlements, while wealth elects officials who will sacrifice today's comfort for tomorrow's children.

Now let's contrast the difference between rich mindsets and wealth mindsets. As I said, *rich* and *wealthy* are two very different things.

1. Rich people get their identity from the things they own: their houses, cars, yachts, money, etc. Wealthy people's identity comes from who they are, not what they own.

2. Rich people either spend a lot of time trying not to lose their money, or spend time wasting it on themselves. Wealthy people's money is just an expression of who they are, so they are confident in their well-being.

3. Rich people work for money, while wealthy people's money works for them.

4. Rich people think of their assets, but wealthy people dream of their legacy.

5. Rich people give to people. Wealthy people invest in people, with the expectation of a return on their investment, measured by a predetermined outcome. Examples are a changed life, a transformed neighborhood, a business profit, etc.

6. Rich people think their money protects them; they have a sense of being above the law. Solomon put it like this: "A rich man's wealth is his strong city, and like a high wall in his own imagination" (Proverbs 18:11). But wealthy people are inherently humble, because they are thankful, knowing that the source of their provision is the Lord.

7. Rich people have a vision for the things they can buy. Wealthy people have a vision for the legacy they are leaving.

8. Rich people compete for money. Wealthy people are compelled by destiny.

9. Rich people step on others to move up. Wealthy people measure success by the people they help up.

10. The rich person's business goal is to make money, whereas a wealthy person's profession yields profit as the fruit of serving others well.

These contrasts are not meant to be the last word on poverty, riches and wealth. They are simple comparisons to help explain how people in each of these mindsets think. They also help explain why many people are rich, but far fewer of them are wealthy. Furthermore, because true wealth is first a condition of the heart that affects the world around you, and is not *necessarily* related to how much money you have in the bank, there are many wealthy people who don't have a lot of assets.

Generosity: The Key to Prosperity

Let's begin to unearth the secrets of the outrageously wealthy and unleash prosperity on your soul. One of the best-kept secrets of the principles of prosperity is generosity, because your generosity determines the capacity of the distribution system that reciprocates your investment in the Kingdom. Let me begin to explain it by quoting Jesus: "Give, and it will be given to you. They will pour into your lap a good measure—pressed down, shaken together, and running over. For by your standard of measure it will be measured to you in return" (Luke 6:38). All prosperity begins with *give*, which means that everybody in the world has the capacity for wealth.

Think about it like this: If prosperity began with *receive* instead of *give*, then each of us would be powerless to produce wealth until someone decided to contribute to our welfare. In other words, it would then be rational to blame your poor condition on the actions of others. But because you initiate all prosperity in your life with *give*, you determine when you will activate your heavenly endowment to receive God's divine power to produce wealth.

"But I grew up in a poor family," you complain, "and I have nothing to give!"

I'm sorry, but you are wrong. Look at the verse again. It does not say, "Give money and it shall be given to you." Jesus just said, "*Give*, and it will be given to you." Everyone has something to give . . . everyone! You can give your time, your gifts, your wisdom, your strength, your encouragement, your talents, etc. You are a treasure chest of true riches, a wealth of benefit to others. Think about what a robot would be worth if it could perform one-tenth of the tasks you are capable of. If you underestimate your ability to *give*, you will undermine your capacity to receive, and thus you could unconsciously relegate your substance to the pig farm instead of the Father's house.

The second part of this verse is equally profound: "For by your standard of measure it will be measured to you in return." Metaphorically speaking, if you give God a teaspoon of rice, He will use your teaspoon (measure) to give you back ten teaspoons of gold. If you give God a bucket of rice, He will use your bucket (measure) to give you back ten buckets of gold.

I heard a beautiful story about rice years ago that illustrates this perfectly. It goes something like this: There was once an old, barefoot peasant walking down the side of a dirt road. He was haggard, destitute, weathered and unkempt, and he was carrying a small wooden bowl of rice. Holding the bowl close to his face, he was carefully scraping each kernel of rice into his mouth with his bare hands. Suddenly, the sound of a hundred horses filled the air. The peasant glanced up from his bowl to observe the commotion.

A thick dust cloud stretched to the heavens, shading the sun's rays from the wretched man's eyes. Yet he perceived through the dust a large, shiny gold chariot encompassed by an entourage of beautiful horses ridden by knights in glistening armor.

As the chariot approached, the ground trembled from the pounding of the horses' hooves, and the cloud of dust covered the peasant's weary head. He pulled his tattered shawl over his weathered face to shield his eyes from the onslaught . . . and maybe to hide his face in shame. He cursed the king's entourage under his breath, grumbling about the gall of the rich man's inconsiderate arrogance. The mere pace of the king's entourage and the breadth of his train stuck in the craw of the poor peasant's heart.

Abruptly, the chariot came to a halt beside the peasant. The old peasant peered carefully through his shawl, waiting for the dust to pass over him. The wealthy king, his crown gleaming with jewels, slowly opened the door of his chariot. The peasant hid his face in shame as the rich king graciously spoke.

"May I have some of your rice, please?" the king requested, to the bewilderment of everyone.

The peasant lifted his shawl over his face, as if retreating into a private inner office to contemplate his situation. As he mumbled something under his breath, his shaky hand emerged reluctantly from beneath his shawl, carefully measuring three kernels of rice into the king's hand.

The king, filled with gratitude, kindly thanked the old peasant. Then he opened his treasure chest and slowly counted out three gold coins, placing each of them carefully in the peasant's outstretched hand.

As the king's entourage began moving again and made its way past the peasant, he ripped off his ragged outer garments, and tossing them to the ground, he yelled, "Oh, that I would have given him the whole bowl of rice!"

I think the moral of the story is pretty clear: Your level of generosity determines the level of God's blessing in your life. The poorer you perceive yourself to be, the more important it is for you to give of yourself.

The Antidote for Poverty

One of the most insightful passages in the entire Bible about destroying the poverty spirit in your life is in the book of Psalms. The psalmist wrote, "Those who sow in tears shall reap with joyful shouting. He who goes to and fro weeping, carrying his bag of seed, shall indeed come again with a shout of joy, bringing his sheaves with him" (Psalm 126:5–6). It would be easy to miss the profound point of this passage. I believe the psalmist is telling the story of someone who needs the very seed he is sowing to feed his children; that is why he is sowing the seed with tears. But he understands that if he does not sow seed when he is broke, then he will have no crop the next season. He knows that he would be destining himself to poverty, since without a crop he would have no income.

In order to change the economic level of your life, you have to give when you are in need, when it is inconvenient, and when you don't feel like it. Let me use the farm story to demonstrate how to *give* your way out of poverty. Let's suppose you have 100 acres of farmland and you plant seed in 50 acres, and then you use the rest of the seed for food. When harvest time comes, you procure a good wheat crop off the 50 acres. The next year, you sacrifice some of the wheat seed you were going to eat, and instead you plant 75 acres of ground. The following year you sacrifice again, but this time you have seed from 75 acres to work with, so you plant the entire 100 acres. The point is simple: The more seed you plant, the more you harvest, and the more you harvest, the more seed you have to plant.

Soon you will have broken the life cycle of poverty by sacrificing today's comfort for tomorrow's prosperity.

Lessons from the Farm

Here are a few more lessons you can learn from the farm:

1. The apostle Paul put it like this: "He who sows sparingly will also reap sparingly, and he who sows bountifully will also reap bountifully" (2 Corinthians 9:6). I think I have already made this point pretty clearly, but because it is the foundation of all prosperity, let me repeat it: Wealth is not determined by what you have; it is predicated on what you give away. Furthermore, the level of your generosity is not measured by the size of anyone else's gift, but by what is left in your care after you give. Jesus taught us this principle when He told a story about a bunch of people giving a lot of money in the Temple. Then a widow came to the offering box and put in two pennies. Jesus said that she gave more than all the rest because she gave everything she had. That is, she had nothing left (see Luke 21:1–4).

2. The next thing you can learn from the farm is that you reap *what* you sow. The Bible says it best: "Do not be deceived, God is not mocked; for whatever a man sows, this he will also reap" (Galatians 6:7). The book of Genesis lays the principle out like this: "The earth brought forth vegetation, plants yielding seed after their kind, and trees bearing fruit with seed in them, after their kind" (Genesis 1:12). If you plant apple seeds, you will not get peach trees. If you are kind to your customers, it will help your business, but it will not fix your marriage. If you give of yourself to people, you will have a wealth of friends, but it probably will

not affect your bank account. I think you get the idea: God created everything after its kind, so you reap *what* you sow. If you need money, then you must sow monetary things into the soil of your desperation to reap an economic harvest of prosperity.

3. It is important to remember that you are always eating last year's crop. Some people live a selfish life for many years and then suddenly decide to be generous. A month later, they are already discouraged because "nothing has happened yet." Changing life cycles is a process that requires patience and perseverance. If you persist, you will prosper in whatever area you sowed into. Remember, God is not mocked—whatever a person sows is what he or she also reaps.

Watchful Insights

I have learned so many of these lessons the hard way. When Kathy and I came to Bethel Church in 1998, we were really broke. But somebody gave me some money for my birthday, and I decided to buy a watch with it. I had never owned nor worn a watch before, because I grew up working on cars, and watches just got in the way. I bought a beautiful Seiko watch that cost $110, which was a lot of money for me at the time.

The next day, we were in church worshiping God when a guy behind me whispered, "Hey, that's a nice watch. Let me see it."

I reluctantly took it off and handed it back to him. A half hour later, the guy handed me his watch and said, "I'll trade you for mine!"

I honestly did not want to trade; I had only owned my watch for less than a day. Not only that, but I liked the way my watched looked a lot better than the way his did. But I did not want to embarrass myself, so after a little haggling, I agreed to the exchange.

A few days later, I took the watch he had traded me to a jewelry store to have the band sized. His watch was too small for my wrist, so I had to have some extra links installed. The salesman who was sizing the band commented on how beautiful the watch was, so I told him, "A guy traded me this watch for my Seiko."

"Wow, you got the better end of that deal!" he said as he reached into a glass case and retrieved a new watch exactly like the one I had brought in. He then showed me the price tag, which read $1,500. "That's a Movado watch; they're pretty expensive," he insisted.

I was so embarrassed by my selfish attitude toward the guy who had traded me watches. I could hardly believe my eyes—I had given the guy a $110 watch, and he had given me a $1,500 watch. Yikes, talk about the great exchange . . . I was stunned!

A year later, I was teaching in Fiji at a YWAM base. When the base leader saw my Movado watch, he fell in love with it. He said jokingly, "I think you're supposed to give me that watch!"

"No way," I joked back. "You're listening to the wrong spirit."

For the next five days we bantered back and forth about my watch, with him insisting I should give it to him. Finally, the night before we were leaving, I heard the Lord tell me to give the guy my watch. I responded, *No way! You gave me this watch!*

The Lord replied, *If you give him your watch, I'll give you a better one.*

The next morning at breakfast, I presented my friend with the watch.

"Oh no, I couldn't take your watch from you," he insisted.

"Shut up, dude. You've been trying to get this watch for five days . . . you're taking it!"

He finally agreed to accept it, and I was happy he did, because before I left Fiji I had a beautiful black-and-gold RADO watch! It was the most awesome timepiece I had ever seen.

Two years passed, and I was in Romania teaching at a couple of conferences with two of my close friends. Romania is a very poor country, and the pastors there barely make enough money to survive. The second day we were there, the Lord told me to give my RADO watch to one of the local pastors.

I asked God, *What deal are You making with me this time?*

No deal! the Lord insisted. *Give the pastor your watch; that's the deal.*

I really loved that watch, and I was not in a financial position to replace it, so I was not excited about giving it away. When I resisted this time, the Lord was not so gracious to me. He said, *When you had a little, you were willing to obey Me, but now that you have a lot, you're disobedient. Don't worry about giving the pastor your watch. I'll just reduce your prosperity down to your ability to obey, and that way you won't be led into temptation.*

I immediately gave the pastor my watch, which brings up a fourth point that is yet another lesson you can learn from the farm:

4. Sometimes the level of your obedience determines the level of your prosperity. Some people believe that if they had a lot, then they would be generous. But Jesus said, "He who is faithful in a very little thing is faithful also in much; and he who is unrighteous in a very little thing is unrighteous also in much" (Luke 16:10). In other words, true wealth is predicated on the generosity of your soul, not on your family lineage, your level of intelligence or your positive personal outlook.

The truth is that every believer is called to be generous, and when you give to God, He gives back to you thirty, sixty and a hundred times more. So if it is true that we are all called to give, and if it is also true that you cannot outgive God, then it stands to reason that all of us are called to be wealthy.

4

Extraordinary
Franchise Opportunities Available

Franchises are one of the most successful ways to start a business, because you are partnering with a company that has systematized a profitable venture that is tried and true. One of the best franchises in American history (rated #2 in the world) is McDonald's. You can buy a McDonald's franchise for somewhere between 1 million and 2 million dollars, plus 8 percent of the gross sales of your business for life. But what I learned recently is that the best franchise in the universe is a heavenly one. That's right! T. D. Jakes helped me understand that God is the Great Franchiser of the universe.

Let me explain. A while back, I turned on the TV just in time to hear T. D. Jakes preaching on tithing in a way that only he can. He had a huge bag of dimes, and he was walking down the aisles of his megachurch and throwing the dimes into the congregation. As near as I can remember, he was shouting something like, *"You can make God your business partner for just ten cents! God has business franchises available for only ten cents. How would you like to be in business with the God of the universe for just ten cents? Brothers and sisters, you would have to be a fool not to want to be in business with the God who knows the future and owns the cattle on a thousand hills!"*

I had already been tithing for thirty years when I heard T. D.'s message, but I did not fully understand the principle I had tapped into. Then while Reverend Jakes was preaching, Scriptures that had been a mystery to me for decades were suddenly revealed to me, like buried treasure hidden in a field. Malachi chapter 3, which was previously one of the most troubling passages in the Bible for me, suddenly made perfect sense. Let's take a close look at it together:

> God said, "Will a man rob God? Yet you are robbing Me! But you say, 'How have we robbed You?' In tithes and offerings. You are cursed with a curse, for you are robbing Me, the whole nation of you! Bring the whole tithe into the storehouse, so that there may be food in My house, and test Me now in this," says the LORD of hosts, "if I will not open for you the windows of heaven and pour out for you a blessing until it overflows. Then I will rebuke the devourer for you, so that it will not destroy the fruits of the ground; nor will your vine in the field cast its grapes," says the LORD of hosts. "All the nations will call you blessed, for you shall be a delightful land," says the LORD of hosts.
>
> Malachi 3:8–12

I understood that God wants us to be generous, and I knew that He honors our giving. But this is different; God is accusing Israel of stealing from Him because they stopped tithing. What's up with that? Then I realized that God had partnered with Israel for their prosperity. Metaphorically speaking, He had franchised the earth out to them. He had provided favorable conditions for their farms to succeed—blessing the soil, causing the rain to fall at the right time, making the sun shine on their crops and so forth. They, on the other hand, had provided the labor—tilling the ground, pruning the vines and harvesting the crops.

God's franchise deal with them was 90/10; the farmers kept 90 percent of the profit, but God, for His part, required the first 10 percent to be His. As the ultimate philanthropist, God wanted His portion of the profits to be given to the priests, who gave spiritual oversight to His people. But the farmers stopped making their franchise payments to God, and instead spent the money on themselves. As you can see from the Scriptures above, our heavenly Father was not very happy about them ripping Him off. In fact, He had already removed the franchised greenhouse effect that caused their crops to produce extraordinary yields and protected their vines from the elements.

I love the way God deals with His franchisees. He says to them, "Test me now in this" (verse 10). In other words, *Give Me back the franchise fee and watch how it affects your crop yields*. He is so gracious and forgiving with them. Even though they have broken their agreement, He promises them that if they make things right with Him, He will add a supernatural element to their farming efforts. This will cause their vines to produce ridiculous yields, so much so that it will dumbfound the surrounding nations.

Questionable Conduct

Let's digress for a moment and talk through some heart issues before we go on. Probably the most frequently asked questions about Kingdom finance are focused on the subject of the tithe. Questions like these come up all the time: "Is the tithe a New Testament principle, or is it relegated to the Old Covenant?" "What, exactly, is the tithe?" "Whom should I give my tithe to, and what's in it for me?"

These are great questions, but before I answer them, I always like to ask the inquiring person, "Are you trying to give *more* or trying to give *less*?" I have been asked these tithing questions more than a hundred times, and only once in twenty years was the person who was doing the inquiring trying to give more. Most often, the people who are debating these questions have other agendas that they are often not even aware of. That said, let me ask you four questions that may help you come to grips with the root cause of any struggle you may have with tithing:

1. *Do you trust God to take care of you?* Here is a great Scripture that will help you move forward in your quest to grow in trusting God: "Trust in the LORD with all your heart and do not lean on your own understanding. In all your ways acknowledge Him, and He will make your paths straight" (Proverbs 3:5–6).

2. *Do you honor the leaders over you who give an account for your life?* The writer of Hebrews gives us insight into the heavy responsibility that God has entrusted to His spiritual leaders. But in an age when family values are being exchanged for independence and even rebellion, this verse feels as if it were written to Martians, or at the least to cavemen: "Obey your leaders and submit to them, for they keep watch over your souls as those who will give an account. Let them do this with joy and not with grief, for this would be unprofitable for you" (Hebrews 13:17). To state the obvious, if you cannot honor your leaders in the sense of trusting them to steward well whatever you give, perhaps you ought to be under different leadership.

3. *Are you serving Mammon (the spirit of greed and materialism) or God? You will always protect the God (or god) you are loyal*

to. Jesus put it best: "No one can serve two masters; for either he will hate the one and love the other, or he will be devoted to one and despise the other. You cannot serve God and wealth" (Matthew 6:24).

4. *Are you afraid of not having enough?* I love the fact that the God of heaven cares about the practical needs we have here on earth. Jesus reassured us that the Father takes care of us with these words: "Do not worry then, saying, 'What will we eat?' or 'What will we drink?' or 'What will we wear for clothing?' For the Gentiles eagerly seek all these things; for your heavenly Father knows that you need all these things" (Matthew 6:31–32).

If you are struggling with the subject of tithing, I want to challenge you right now to put down this book and ask the Holy Spirit to search your heart. Ask Him if your resistance is really rooted in the theology of the tithe, or if there are deeper issues that trouble you. Let Him lead you into all truth and deliver you from poverty, the fear of lack and the need for control.

In the Beginning

It has always astonished me that the God of the universe actually has any interest in humans giving Him gifts at all, much less money. If you are God, what are you going to do with the stuff? It is not as though there is a grocery store or supermarket or something that God visits. If He wants anything, He just speaks and it is His: "Let there be Pepsi. . . ." And *bam* . . . He is drinking a cold one! So what's up with giving to God?

That is a great question, yet there is one thing that God wants but which He cannot make happen—to be loved freely. God gave

75

us a free will so that He could experience us freely giving our love to Him. Love, by its very nature, requires freedom of choice. Love forced or love programmed is not love at all. God is love, which means He has the capacity both to give love and to be loved. Because love "believes all things," our trusting in God is a manifestation of loving Him (1 Corinthians 13:7). God can discern a gift that is given out of obligation or manipulation from a gift that is rooted in love. This is evidenced in the story of Cain and Abel. Here is a short account:

> So it came about in the course of time that Cain brought an offering to the LORD of the fruit of the ground. Abel, on his part also brought of the firstlings of his flock and of their fat portions. And the LORD had regard for Abel and for his offering; but for Cain and for his offering He had no regard.
>
> Genesis 4:3–5

A few things come to light in this story. First, the *need* to give back to God is deeply rooted in human nature, so much so that Cain received no sympathy for giving God a crummy offering, even though he did it without God asking for it. I think that God had no regard for Cain's offering because He had no respect for Cain's motives. In other words, God refused to be manipulated by Cain's gift. It is like having a teenage son who is in complete rebellion against you, and then he picks some old, wilted flowers out of your garden and hands them to you. You would be thinking, *What's the catch? What is he trying to bribe me into doing?*

Unlike Cain, Abel gave God the first and best of his flock as a precious gift, and God *loved it*. Here lies the beauty of our wonderful Creator basking in the love of His mere mortal creature, giving Abel a pathway of expression to unleash the passion that gushed

76

within him for his God. More than a thousand years before Moses ever wrote the Law that required the people of God to give their Creator the first and the best, Abel already was loving God freely with his extravagant gift.

Tithing into Eternity

Now let's journey forward several hundred years, to the days of Abraham. It is about 2000 BC, several centuries before Moses would carry the Ten Commandments down from Mount Sinai. Abraham and his nephew Lot agree to go their own separate ways to settle a conflict between their herdsmen. Lot and his people go down to the city of Sodom and settle there, while Abraham settles in the land of Canaan (see Genesis 13). Time passes and a war breaks out between several cities, which results in the city of Sodom being ransacked and its citizens being taken into captivity. When Abraham hears about the plight of Sodom and the captivity of his nephew Lot, he gathers 318 of his men and sets out to rescue the city. Miraculously, Abraham defeats five attacking kings with his small band of warriors and liberates Sodom, ultimately freeing Lot and his family from the clutches of the enemy (see Genesis 14:1–16).

This is a pretty wild story, right? But wait, it gets better. Suddenly, a man who has no beginning and no end (yes, you read that right) steps out onto the battlefield. His name is Melchizedek, and he greets Abraham with some bread and wine. Abraham gives this mystery man a tenth of all the spoil he has recovered from the battle (see Genesis 14:17–24). But the author of the book of Hebrews says that when Abraham tithed to Melchizedek, Levi also tithed to him (see Hebrews 7:1–10). At first glance this seems pretty vanilla, until you realize that at the point when Abraham gave that tithe, Levi was yet to be born. He would not be born for another three generations! A man tithed who had not even been born yet, but he received a blessing because he was the great-grandson of Abraham.

Let me put this together for you: Abraham tithes to Melchizedek, who lives in eternity (he has no beginning and no end), so he reaps a legacy in that his great-grandson gets credit for his great-grandfather's righteous generosity. Levi has inherited multigenerational favor simply by being the descendant of a man who lived with eternal values.

This story illustrates three important facts about tithing. First of all, Abraham tithed to God several centuries before the Law of Moses required it. This, of course, demonstrates that the tithe precedes the Law. Second, Abraham is called the "father of faith," as he "believed God, and it was reckoned to him as righteousness" (Galatians 3:6). Abraham tithed by faith, not out of obligation. And third, Abraham's tithe positively impacted the generations after him because the tithe is an eternal principle.

God Lays Down the Law

Have you ever had someone give you a gift that you really could not use? Sure, we all have. I am certain that is where we get the expression "it's the thought that counts." As we see throughout the Bible, righteous people gave God gifts, and their beautiful heart of generosity blessed Him. But when Moses came along and received the Law, God decided to give His people a glimpse into how much He desired their generosity.

I kind of think of it like a bride and groom who set up a wedding registry at a department store so that those who wish to give to them will know what the newlyweds actually want. Likewise, God outlined a very detailed description of His desire for His people's generosity. For the scope of this book, I will break it down into four simple principles. The first couple of principles for the tithe, both found in the same verse, are foundational: "Thus all the tithe of the land, of the seed of the land or of the fruit of the tree, is the LORD's; it is holy to the LORD" (Leviticus 27:30). Many other verses contained in the Law of Moses repeat these two principles, but here they are in a nutshell:

1. God wants 10 percent of all our income to be given to Him.
2. Whatever we give to God becomes holy.

It is remarkable to me that the fruit of our labor, typically expressed through currency, becomes immediately holy when it is transferred to the Lord's work. Think about it like this: I could be holding a $100 bill that was once used to buy illegal drugs, and then later was used to pay for prostitution. But as soon as I give it to the Lord, that same currency is suddenly sanctified to the work of the King and His Kingdom.

The third principle is the main directive God gave His people about the use of the tithe: "For the tithe of the sons of Israel, which they offer as an offering to the LORD, I have given to the Levites for an inheritance; therefore I have said concerning them, 'They shall have no inheritance among the sons of Israel'" (Numbers 18:24).

3. The Levites who ministered to the people of God were to receive the tithe as income and inheritance. The Levites were the ones who had the responsibility of pastoring/shepherding the people of God. God tasked them with watching over the souls of their people and guiding them into wholeness. Our spiritual leaders have this role in our lives in the New Testament, as I pointed out earlier from Hebrews 13:17.

The fourth principle expands on the idea that God wants the tithe to be brought into the storehouse: "'Bring the whole tithe into the storehouse, so that there may be food in My house, and test Me now in this,' says the LORD of hosts, 'if I will not open for you the windows of heaven and pour out for you a blessing until it overflows'" (Malachi 3:10).

4. The storehouse is a reference to the storehouse of wisdom that is supposed to flow from the priests who feed the people spiritual food.

The author of the book of Hebrews echoed this kind of language when he exhorted his people: "For though by this time you ought to be teachers, you have need again for someone to teach you the elementary principles of the oracles of God, and you have come to need milk and not solid food" (Hebrews 5:12). The word *food* in the Hebrew language can be translated "freshly torn prey," which is a great metaphor for spiritual revelation. God was basically saying to His people, *You are robbing Me, and therefore there is no food [spiritual revelation] in My house.* This would be true of any of us who withhold the tithe.

In other words, when we give natural gifts to God, He gives us back spiritual gifts. It is no coincidence, then, that Judas, who literally stole from the offerings and practically lived with Jesus, seemed to have no idea that Jesus was the Messiah. There was no spiritual revelation (freshly torn prey) in his soul, because there was no generosity in his heart.

On the other hand, Mary poured perfume worth a year's wages over Jesus, and He said she was preparing Him for burial. None of the disciples seemed to understand this, but Mary understood it. She gave extravagantly to God, and He gave her back spiritual revelation. Jesus went on to say that the story of her extravagant generosity would be shared every place the Gospel was preached.

Jesus Taught Tithing

Now let's bring the tithe into the New Covenant. The Pharisees, who were notorious for doing things to appear holy, but who were really full of evil motives, ran into a buzz saw with Jesus. He proclaimed, "But woe to you Pharisees! For you pay tithe of mint and rue and every kind of garden herb, and yet disregard justice and the love of God; but these are the things you should have done without neglecting the others" (Luke 11:42).

The Pharisees practiced the "Cain giving method," which, as we saw earlier, had already been tried and had failed miserably. They gave gifts to God, but they did not love Him, nor did they deal honestly with people. Yet even in the midst of their treachery, Jesus told them that they should not neglect tithing, but that they must deal with their motives.

Let's bring it all home by answering a few of the tithing questions this chapter raises. To start, what is a tithe? The word *tithe* means "ten," as in 10 percent of your income. One of the most important principles of the tithe, however, is that it is not just 10 percent—it is the *first* 10 percent. In other words, God challenges you to pay your tithe before you pay your bills or spend money on anything else. Remember, the Old Testament saints were to give the *first fruits* of their fields (see Exodus 23:16). In this way, you are tithing by *faith* in that you are giving God His share before you deal with your purchases or expenses. Thus, you must trust Him to provide for the rest of your needs and desires. This is one of the key elements that establishes the tithe as a New Testament principle—you are giving by faith, not by Law.

The tithe is not a gift, either. It is your "franchise payment" for God's partnership in your life—the most extraordinary franchise opportunity that will ever come your way. In other words, you owe

God the tithe. Furthermore, the tithe is to be *paid* to the storehouse (typically your church), the place that provides you with spiritual meat and milk. You don't get to designate your tithe to a certain activity or person. It is not yours; it is God's. Therefore, you cannot control it. If you ask God to partner with you in life and you don't pay God His 10 percent dividend, He calls it robbery. You have basically ripped off your business partner and embezzled your stockholder's money.

When you give money above the tithe, which is everything above 10 percent, it is called an *offering*. Your generosity begins above the tithe. You have the freedom to give an offering to anyone or anywhere you want. God has given you authority over 90 percent of your income to do with as you see fit. He wants you to be as generous with your money (the 90 percent) as He is with His portion.

God Cares What You Do

Contrary to popular opinion, God cares what you do with your money. When Jesus went to church (the Temple), He sat next to the offering box so He could watch what people put in the offering. When a widow put all she had into the offering (although it was just two copper coins), Jesus made a major issue out of it. He called His disciples over and said, "Truly I say to you, this poor widow put in more than all the contributors to the treasury" (Mark 12:43).

A few years after the resurrection, a community of new believers was so touched by God that its people became ridiculously generous with one another. They began selling their houses and property to meet the needs of the poor among them. They laid their money at the apostles' feet, trusting them to distribute the money as they saw fit. In other words, they were extremely generous, but they also trusted their leaders' wisdom to sow their money into the right people more than they trusted themselves. The result was that "there was not a needy person among them" (Acts 4:34).

A couple named Ananias and Sapphira got caught up in the peer pressure of their community to give sacrificially, so they sold a piece of land they owned. They brought a portion of the money from the sale and gave it to the apostles to distribute. But they lied about their gift by representing their offering as an extravagant "we gave it all" kind of gift, when in fact it was only a portion of their sales price. Peter, knowing by the Holy Spirit that they were lying their faces off, confronted them individually about their deception. Unfortunately, neither of them came clean, so the Holy Spirit ended their lives immediately and they both dropped dead on the spot (see Acts 5:1–11). Yikes, that will scare the heck out of you! God is watching us, and He cares what we do with our money.

Building Monuments in Heaven

Let's fast-forward about five more years in the book of Acts and meet a man from Caesarea named Cornelius. The guy is a Roman centurion. Look how Acts 10:1–4 describes him:

> Now there was a man at Caesarea named Cornelius, a centurion of what was called the Italian cohort, a devout man and one who feared God with all his household, and gave many alms to the Jewish people and prayed to God continually. About the ninth hour of the day he clearly saw in a vision an angel of God who had just come in and said to him, "Cornelius!" And fixing his gaze on him and being much alarmed, he said, "What is it, Lord?" And he said to him, "Your prayers and alms have ascended as a memorial before God."

This encounter resulted in one of the most extraordinary, supernatural stories in the entire Bible. The angel tells Cornelius to send some men to a house where the apostle Peter is staying by the sea, in a city called Joppa. He tells him to ask Peter to come share the Gospel with his entire family. While Cornelius is having this angelic encounter about Peter, Peter falls into a trance and has a God encounter about Cornelius. Just as Peter comes out of the trance, the centurion's men are at the door, asking to talk to him. Ultimately, Peter goes with the men to Cornelius's house, where he finds the centurion's entire family waiting for him. Peter begins unpacking the Gospel to them, but while he is still preaching, the Holy Spirit falls on Cornelius's family and they all get filled with the Holy Spirit. Of course, this results in this whole Gentile family getting saved and baptized in water.

What a great story, but did you notice how it all began? A Gentile guy—a man who does not know God personally, but does fear Him—is praying to Him and giving offerings to the Jewish people. Remember that the angel said to Cornelius that his alms (giving) had created a memorial in heaven? God often commanded His people to set up memorials to Him so that they would remember His works in their lives. For example, when Joshua crossed the Jordan River on dry land, God told him to take rocks from the middle of the river and build a memorial out of them. Joshua told the people,

> Let this be a sign among you, so that when your children ask later, saying, "What do these stones mean to you?" then you shall say to them, "Because the waters of the Jordan were cut off before the ark of the covenant of the LORD; when it crossed the Jordan, the waters of the Jordan were cut off." So these stones shall become a memorial to the sons of Israel forever.
>
> Joshua 4:6–7

So, we are to build memorials to the works of God on earth. Yet what moves me is that God is setting up memorials in heaven to remember our generosity and our prayers. Think about it: Your tithes and offerings are building monuments in heaven and are laying a foundation for God to move at the perfect time in your life and in the lives of your family. God cares, God sees and God rewards what you do with your money.

5

The Legacy of Prosperity

On May 12, 1780, John Adams, the second president of the United States of America, wrote a letter to his beloved wife, Abigail, that will forever mark him as one of the greatest visionaries of all time. He said,

> I must study politics and war that my sons may have liberty to study mathematics and philosophy. My sons ought to study mathematics and philosophy, geography, natural history, naval architecture, navigation, commerce and agriculture, in order to give their children a right to study painting, poetry, music, architecture, statuary, tapestry and porcelain.[1]

John Adams's understanding of how legacies are supposed to evolve is not just insightful; it is profound. His explanation of the responsibility that each generation has to leave an inheritance to future generations is at the very core of the heart of God Himself. The Kingdom of God is by its very nature metamorphosing, expanding and increasing in its influence, power and glory from generation to generation. In fact, about 2,700 years ago the great prophet Isaiah spoke of the perpetually expanding nature of God's world. He proclaimed, "There will be no end to the increase of His government or of peace" (Isaiah 9:7). The words of Jesus echoed this notion when He said, "Truly, truly, I say to you, he who believes in Me, the works that I do, he will do also; and greater works than these he will do; because I go to the Father" (John 14:12).

This Generation

The goal of joining the generations is that the next generation would embrace the core values of the previous generations and then build on them. This twenty-first-century generation is the most creative, innovative and inventive generation ever to have graced this planet. They will cure cancer, eradicate poverty and create a global community that embraces and perpetuates peace . . . or they will utterly fail.

Allow me to expound on my perspectives with a personal story. Christmas has always been the most celebrated holiday in our family. We did not have a lot of money when our kids were growing up, but we always did our best to make sure that each of our children had at least one really great gift under the Christmas tree. Now we have eight grandchildren, and our financial situation has improved dramatically. My writing books and speaking at conferences all over the world has enriched our family substantially, so that we can afford pretty much anything our grandchildren desire. This has led to some interesting family dynamics in the last ten years. Christmas is one of the places where this newfound wealth has manifested the most. Our celebrations have taken on sort of an air-of-prosperity that at times seems a little overboard and dysfunctional to me.

The whole thing came to a climax at Christmas 2012. That year, each of our children and grandchildren gave Kathy a "Christmas want list," as has been our tradition for more than three decades. But unlike most years, where Kathy would sift through the list and choose a few things for each person, she instead decided to get them everything on all their lists. By the time Christmas Day arrived, the tree had literally disappeared beneath the gifts that were stacked to the ceiling, not to mention another pile of presents nearly as big downstairs.

Like always, the night before Christmas our entire family slept at our house. Morning came early as the grandkids woke everyone up with their playful anticipation. Our grandkids were so excited that nobody even had time to brush their teeth. We finally gathered around the Christmas tree and began to tell the Baby Jesus story. Each of us took turns at telling the story, with each person's narration building on the next. The narrative concluded and I began to give out the gifts, calling out names as we distributed the packages from person to person in a kind of human chain. Nearly two hours passed as wrapping paper slowly filled every empty spot on the floor.

Suddenly, a whimper to my left broke ranks with our laughter . . . the room grew strangely silent. I noticed that my daughter was whispering a strong correction to one of her children. This child got up from the floor, cheeks streaming with tears, and stumbled through the wrapping paper, mumbling defiantly all the way to the bedroom. My daughter ordered her young one to "stay there until you change your attitude," and the door slammed shut in response.

I immediately questioned the child's mother to determine what had caused the outburst, and I learned that "Grandma missed one gift" from the child's Christmas list.

"But we bought the kid fifteen presents!" I protested.

"I know, Dad. Don't worry about it," my daughter responded.

Meanwhile, Kathy retreated to our office and a minute later re-emerged with her Christmas lists in her hand. "I did forget one gift," she said with compassion. "I'm so sorry," she explained, while choking back tears. Trying to smooth the situation over, she added, "I'll go tomorrow and buy the gift I missed."

The rest of the family joined in on my protest, reassuring her that the child needed to get over it.

I was furious inside but I kept my mouth shut, not wanting to ruin Christmas for everyone else. However, Christmas was wrecked for me! I could not go to sleep that night. I just lay there reflecting on my grandchild's attitude and musing over our failure to instill gratitude in them. In our quest to bless our family, we had unknowingly sown seeds of entitlement into the soil of their little hearts for years. I determined to fix the problem. I wanted no part in raising spoiled brats who would grow up to become monetary monsters!

Kathy and I decided that Christmas 2013 was going to be different. We would atone for the transgressions of the past holidays and begin to instill gratitude into our beautiful, young, ungrateful creatures. Our plan was to buy them each one great gift. But most importantly, we decided to choose some extremely poor families with children and have our grandkids buy gifts for them (with our money), and then deliver them on Christmas Day.

The plan worked perfectly; I had our outreach team pick three of the most destitute families with young children in our city. We found out the names and ages of the kids and bought a bunch of gifts for all of them.

When Christmas Day finally arrived, we loaded up the gifts and drove to the apartment complex to give the presents to the children. Upon arrival, we worked our way through the trash that covered the front yard, and we went up the stairs that led to the first apartment. The air was filled with the smell of cigarette smoke as we walked single file, navigating several people sitting on the steps and staring at us. All seven of the grandkids we had at the time stood silently at the front door of the first apartment, afraid of what might emerge from its entrance. I lined up all the grandkids facing the door, gifts in hand, and knocked. A few seconds passed before the door opened, squeaking in resistance against its rusted hinges. Smoke poured out over the threshold as a maybe forty-year-old woman emerged from a dark, smoky room. Her hair was matted and unkempt, her eyes were drawn back into her thin face, and she was wearing an old pink bathrobe.

"Merry Christmas!" we all shouted in unison. Suddenly, eight little kids ten years old and under rushed the door from the inside, fighting for who was going to get out first. Our kids sheepishly handed them their gifts as they excitedly searched for their names on each present. All of us watched with our hearts in our throats as they hurried back into the front room, where the floor was covered in wall-to-wall mattresses. They ripped the wrapping paper off their gifts like wild dogs after wounded prey . . . laughing and screaming as each present was unveiled. We just stood there speechless, trying to wrap our brains around the intense pain, which was somehow intermingled with this peculiar joy our hearts were experiencing. A few more awkward minutes passed before we said our good-byes and slowly pried ourselves away from the door.

The scene repeated itself two more times that afternoon as we completed our Christmas mission. It is hard to explain my grandchildren's moods as we got in our cars and headed back to the house to finish our own gift exchange. But it should suffice to say that they never complained about their gifts again!

The challenge with John Adams's vision of each generation building on the next generation's accomplishments is that those who make up the current generation often forget the sacrifice it took to give them such an amazing inheritance. They tend not to value it because they did not work for it, and consequently, they don't do what is necessary to sustain it. In fact, they often don't know what to do to sustain the culture they inherited, because they were not there when it was built.

An attitude of thanksgiving is the only effective inoculation against entitlement and pride. Yet thanksgiving must be inspired in its recipients proactively by remembering and recounting the perseverance and sacrifice of others. The moment we lose sight of the historic exploits of our forefathers and foremothers, we begin to digress into the cesspool of "privileged thinking," and inheritance becomes entitlement.

Instant Gratification Generation

One of the worst side effects of entitlement is the instant gratification culture it inspires—the sense that we should get what we want when we want it, regardless of our circumstances. This instant gratification mentality is expressed in hundreds of ways in our society. Credit cards and thirty-year mortgages are just a couple of ways that this attitude finds expression. Of course, I am not saying these things in themselves are evil or bad; I am simply pointing out that they are expressions of a culture full of people who want it *now*, regardless of whether they can afford it or not. Think about it: Credit cards have only been around for about fifty years. That means our great-grandparents actually had to have money to buy things. I know it seems ridiculous to us now, but it is true.

One of the challenges of the instant gratification culture is that it can take away the motivation we have to persevere through tough times in order to apprehend our aspirations, because we can just charge it. Slowly but surely, perseverance is becoming a lost art, shared by few and passed on to no one. In a strange way, our supernatural culture can even feed our impatient obsession in that we believe in miracles, which is the immediate intervention of God in a situation. This can undermine our value of life's processes that are often rooted in perseverance.

The truth is, God often takes a long time to act suddenly. As a matter of fact, many of the most amazing "instant miracles" I have witnessed have been predicated by years of prayer and persistent faithfulness. This reminds me of the story Jesus told about the widow who wore out the wicked judge with her persistence:

> Now He was telling them a parable to show that at all times they ought to pray and not to lose heart, saying, "In a certain city there was a judge who did not fear God and did not respect man. There was a widow in that city, and she kept coming to him, saying, 'Give me legal protection from my opponent.' For a while he was unwilling; but afterward he said to himself, 'Even though I do not fear God nor respect man, yet because this widow bothers me, I will give her legal protection, otherwise by continually coming she will wear me out.'" And the Lord said, "Hear what the unrighteous judge said; now, will not God bring about justice for His elect who cry to Him day and night, and will He delay long over them? I tell you that He will bring about justice for them quickly. However, when the Son of Man comes, will He find faith on the earth?"
>
> Luke 18:1–8

The reason Jesus told His guys this parable was to keep them from wimping out in prayer by quitting before they got answers. Jesus closes with a profound question about whether or not, when He returns, He will "find faith on the earth." The connotation is that persistent, prolonged, unyielding, "I refuse to give up" prayer is *faith*.

The point is, if persistence and perseverance are rooted in faith, then the instant gratification "I have to have it now" mentality must be inspired by the wrong kingdom. Furthermore, perseverance is not a gift, or even a personality type; it is a choice that we make to refuse to give up when life gets tough. The fruit of perseverance is great character and promise actualized. In fact, perseverance is to our soul what exercise is to our body. When we push against the challenges of life, our inner man gains strength day by day. On the other hand, when we act like impatient, entitled, spoiled victims, our inner man degenerates, leaving our new man withered, weak and pitiful.

Growing Greatness

If we are to realize John Adams's dream of perpetually advancing the generations, we must instill nobility into the hearts of the generations that follow us. But many people cannot move forward in life because they are fixed on their past failures. They spend all their time regretting their mistakes and punishing themselves instead of receiving the forgiveness of Jesus into their lives. They need to get past their past! We can help them by inspiring them with vision for the future, so that they don't look back in shame while they are faithfully plowing their own pastures of prosperity. Jesus said it like this: "No one, after putting his hand to the plow and looking back, is fit for the kingdom of God" (Luke 9:62). People who continually look back while tilling their field of dreams will never be fulfilled, because they have sacrificed their future on the regrets of their past.

When we keep our eyes on the task before us, hope and faith begin to rise in our hearts. It is hope that "feels" a deep sense of destiny, and faith that "sees" the promises long before they are actualized, which ultimately fuels perseverance in our inner man. P. K. Bernard said it best: "A man without a vision is a man without a future. A man without a future will always return to his past."

Like Adam and Eve, we have been invited to eat from the Tree of Life and live forever. (Jesus is our Tree of Life, metaphorically speaking.) It is only when we focus intently on the Tree of Life that we lose our appetite for the instant gratification fruit tree. In other words, it is our *Big Yes* in life—the passion we have for righteous dreams—that helps us resist the temptation of the world. But metaphorically speaking, if we attempt to sterilize our environment by cutting down the Tree of Knowledge of Good and Evil in our garden (i.e., our life), we actually undermine our opportunities to resist temptation and to grow our character through perseverance. An ancient proverb explains it like this: "Smooth seas don't produce skillful sailors."

To summarize, we want to create a culture where each generation can live in the Kingdom that is advancing from glory to greater glory. This is the ultimate desire of the Father Himself. Yet to live successfully in greater abundance around us, we must increase our capacity for a greater glory within ourselves. Otherwise, like my grandchildren whose hearts began to be infected by the spirit of entitlement, we digress into the cesspool of the spirit of entitlement.

It is gratitude and perseverance that inspire hope and faith within us. These attributes and attitudes inoculate us from evil and expand our capacity for greater blessing in our inner man. I want to challenge you, therefore, to resist the temptation to take the easy road. Instead, take the highway of perseverance, which will become the path to your palace. This is the process of nobility that prepares us to embrace our royal identity and fulfill our divine destiny.

6

Money Is *Not* a Measure
of Spirituality, Unless It Is!

One of the most destructive heresies of the twentieth century was what some theologians termed the "prosperity gospel." This theology was rooted in the idea that spirituality was measured by one's outward display of wealth or riches. Many well-meaning believers swallowed this teaching hook, line and sinker, which created intense peer pressure to appear prosperous.

Fine clothes, fancy cars, expensive homes and even private jets were common manifestations of the prosperity gospel. Yet most of it was a house of cards financed by massive debt and perpetuated by smoke and mirrors, pride and vanity, arrogance and egotism. The standing joke was, "He left for work in a $75,000 Mercedes and came home in a $750,000 bus!" In other words, the guy bought an expensive car to impress people and could not even make the payments on it. Consequently, he ended up having to take the bus home after they repoed his car.

But worse than the paper-thin prosperity was the fact that character often surrendered itself to pleasure and gratification, while sacrifice and perseverance went AWOL. To be fair, not everyone who taught the prosperity gospel embraced these clear abuses of Scripture; there were some teachers who took a more balanced approach to wealth. Nevertheless, there was enough abuse that it caused many prominent leaders to brand the teaching as heresy.

Life Lessons from Abraham

Bill Johnson has said, "When we react, instead of respond, to an abuse, we often create a worse doctrine than the one we reacted to!" This is true of the prosperity gospel. We have thrown out the proverbial baby with the bathwater and lost some of the most profound realities of the Bible. Let's journey way back in time to the days of Abraham, whom Scriptures call the "father of faith," and see if we can embrace the truth about wealth from our founding father. Abraham did not have a Bible, because he lived four hundred years before Moses, who penned the first five books of the Torah (Bible). Abraham did not have a church or even a men's group to go to; there were none to go to in those days. But Abraham did have a unique relationship with God, in which God called him His "friend forever" (see 2 Chronicles 20:7). One of the benefits or manifestations of Abraham's relationship with God is that he was "very rich in livestock, in silver and in gold" (Genesis 13:2).

Abraham was extremely cautious about who got credit for his fortune. When he conquered those warring kings, as we talked about in chapter 4, and he rescued Sodom, along with Lot and his family, the king of Sodom was so grateful that he tried to give Abraham all the riches of the city. But Abraham said to him, "I have sworn to the LORD God Most High, possessor of heaven and earth, that I will not take a thread or a sandal thong or anything that is yours, for fear you would say, 'I have made Abram rich'" (Genesis 14:22–23).

I am pointing out here that not only was Abraham rich, but he also attributed his wealth to God alone. In other words, God made Abraham rich—period. Case closed. There is no other way to view his prosperity. In fact, Abraham was not just rich; he had a trophy wife named Sarah. Sarah was so beautiful that even at ninety years old, when she and Abraham journeyed through various countries, the kings would hear about her beauty and try to abduct her so they could marry her.

Oh no! This is already starting to *sound* like the prosperity gospel. But read on, because it has a completely different heart.

Wealth Is a Family Affair

Abraham and Sarah had a son named Isaac, and although he was never called a friend of God, he also had a thing about wealth. The Bible puts it like this:

> Now Isaac sowed in that land and reaped in the same year a hundred-fold. And the LORD blessed him, and the man became rich, and continued to grow richer until he became very wealthy; for he had possessions of flocks and herds and a great household, so that the Philistines envied him.
>
> Genesis 26:12–14

Like his father, Isaac also had a trophy wife. Rebekah was so beautiful that she too was abducted by a king. Talk about the lifestyle of the rich and famous! Abraham and his extended family had all the makings of a soap opera, except that they all loved God. God prospered

99

them, but the people around them were jealous and consequently hated them for it. Nothing ever changes!

Fast-forward another twenty years. Isaac and Rebekah gave birth to their twins, Esau, who was the older by a few minutes, and Jacob. Through an elaborate conspiracy between Rebekah and her son Jacob, the twins' father blessed him instead of Esau, which released some sort of supernatural wealth on the young man.

A while later, Jacob fell in love with a woman named Rachel, whom he met at a well. He worked for her father, Laban, for seven years as a dowry. But on the honeymoon night, Laban slipped Leah, Rachel's older sister, into the bridal chamber, and Jacob ended up consummating the marriage with Leah instead of Rachel. Laban credited Jacob's seven years of work to Leah, and then he required Jacob to work seven more years to pay off the dowry for Rachel (see Genesis 29:1–30). I know, I know . . . you just cannot make this stuff up!

But wait, the story gets even crazier. God was with Jacob, and everything he touched turned to gold. Jacob finally got fed up with Laban's deceit and tried to quit. But Laban knew that Jacob was making him a fortune, so he cut a deal with him that seemed fair on the surface. It turned out, however, to be Laban's demise. The contract called for Jacob to get all the spotted and speckled sheep and goats, and for Laban to own all the solid-colored flock. This is where the story becomes otherworldly. Jacob went down to the watering hole where all the sheep and goats mated, and when the strong sheep and goats were mating, he put spotted and speckled branches in front of them. Consequently, all the strong sheep and goats were born spotted and speckled, while the feeble and weak of the flock were solid-colored and so belonged to Laban. Over the next few years, the Lord transferred the wealth of Laban to Jacob, until Jacob became extremely rich (see Genesis 30:25–43).

After twenty years, Jacob left his father-in-law's place with his two wives and all his flock. On his journey, he had an encounter with an angel at a place called Jabbok, in which the angel changed his name from Jacob, which means "deceiver" in Hebrew, to Israel, which means "a prince with God" (see Genesis chapters 32–33). Jacob had twelve sons through his two wives, Leah and Rachel, and his two concubines. God so blessed Jacob/Israel that he became the father of a nation. How would you like to become so wealthy, favored and powerful that you become your own nation?

From Family Affair to National Anointing

The anointing for wealth that began with Abraham, and later passed to Isaac and Jacob, became a national anointing that actually rested on the entire nation of Israel. Let's fast-forward a few centuries, this time to the days of Moses. God spoke through Moses in the wilderness and said to the people, "You shall remember the LORD your God, for it is He who is giving you power to make wealth, that He may confirm His covenant which He swore to your fathers, as it is this day" (Deuteronomy 8:18).

Wow! There are two things that grab me from this passage. The first is that God gave His people power to make wealth. In other words, wealth is more than wise financial investments; it is actually a magnetic force—a tractor beam, so to speak—that sucks prosperity into its vortex. When God anoints a person, or in this case an entire nation, with the power to make wealth, it creates an invisible yet tangible culture in which people feel impassioned to give to those who are anointed, even though they often cannot even explain why. This kind of anointing transcends logic and reason. Its influence often appeals more to the heart (spirit) than it does the head. People often feel an overwhelming need to give to people with this anointing.

We all feel compelled to give to a person in dire need—a homeless person or a hungry child, for example. Situations like these awaken compassion in us to meet a pressing need. There are other times that someone shares a vision so compelling that we are inspired to contribute to see the vision fulfilled. Our contributions in these cases can be traced back to something logical, explainable and natural. But the power to make wealth cannot be explained by circumstances alone, nor is it just people's response to a highly motivational speaker or even a great vision. It is, instead, a spiritual power endowed by our Creator, which requires a divine response from creation itself to fulfill His heavenly decree.

Furthermore, the power to make wealth does not just affect the generosity of others; it actually affects creation itself. Think about how Isaac sowed in the land and reaped a hundredfold. The land—creation itself—was compelled by the prosperity tractor beam of God to yield its best to Isaac.

What I am saying is that the elements of nature are somehow required to respond to this supernatural attraction. And it gets even better. This power to make wealth also supernaturally affects man-made financial conditions and situations like the stock market, business deals and customer sales. Many of the people God has anointed to make wealth do have extraordinary financial minds, but the mere frequency of their success is uncanny and incomprehensible. They often prosper against ridiculous odds.

The second part of this verse that I find so compelling is the purpose behind the power to make wealth. God said the purpose is "that He may confirm His covenant which He swore to your fathers, as it is this day." In this case, wealth is actually a sign of God's blessing on a person's life, or on a city or a nation's life. This is where the prosperity gospel really gets dicey, because most of us want to believe that wealth has nothing to do with spirituality. But according to Moses, sometimes prosperity has everything to do with your relationship with God. In fact, some people are wealthy *because* they know God.

I am sorry; I know how hard this is to hear, especially if you are broke and are a faithful lover of Jesus. But it happens to be 100 percent true. Before you freak out, let's make sure you understand what I am and am not saying. I am not saying that rich people necessarily know God, nor am I proposing that God gives them their wealth. Neither am I suggesting that God does not bless poor people. Yet in the midst of trying to navigate these two extremes, I am pointing out that there is a third option. God does often bless certain people with the power to make wealth. Their wealth is, therefore, a sign of their relationship with Him.

Inspired by the Rich and Famous

The life of King Solomon is the most profound story ever told about God's extraordinary power to make a person rich beyond comprehension. The story began right after King David died and Solomon became king in his place. Solomon went to the worship center at Gibeon, where the tent of meeting was pitched, and he worshiped God with reckless abandon. The guy literally sacrificed a thousand sheep to God in one day. (Aren't you thankful that you live in the New Covenant, where radical worship is not measured by the number of sheep you offer God?) When Solomon got home that night, God appeared to him and said, *What do you want from Me? Ask for anything* (see 2 Chronicles 1:1–7). Look at Solomon's request and God's answer:

> Solomon answered, "You were extravagantly generous with David my father, and now you have made me king in his place. Establish, GOD, the words you spoke to my father, for you've given me a staggering

task, ruling this mob of people. Yes, give me wisdom and knowledge as I come and go among this people—for who on his own is capable of leading these, your glorious people?"

God answered Solomon, "This is what has come out of your heart: You didn't grasp for money, wealth, fame, and the doom of your enemies; you didn't even ask for a long life. You asked for wisdom and knowledge so you could govern well my people over whom I've made you king. Because of this, you get what you asked for—wisdom and knowledge. And I'm presenting you the rest as a bonus—money, wealth, and fame beyond anything the kings before or after you had or will have."

2 Chronicles 1:8–12 message

The Bible goes on to say, "The king made silver and gold as common as rocks, and cedar as common as the fig trees in the lowland hills" (2 Chronicles 1:14–17 message). Imagine how wealthy a person would have to be for gold and silver to be as common as rocks. But the real point here is that God made Solomon unfathomably rich. The question that intrigues me the most is, *How* did God make him rich? Did God supernaturally turn dirt into gold, like Jesus when He turned water into wine? Or did coins suddenly appear in the mouths of fish, as was also the case in the days of Christ?

The answer to these questions is unequivocally no. At least four factors marked Solomon's wealth: supernatural wisdom, favor, excellence and creativity. All these attributes were on full display when the queen of Sheba made her famous visit to Solomon's palace. Look at her reaction:

When the queen of Sheba experienced for herself Solomon's wisdom and saw with her own eyes the palace he had built, the meals that were served, the impressive array of court officials and sharply dressed waiters, the lavish crystal, and the elaborate worship extravagant with Whole-Burnt-Offerings at the steps leading up to The Temple of GOD, it took her breath away.

She said to the king, "It's all true! Your reputation for accomplishment and wisdom that reached all the way to my country is confirmed. I wouldn't have believed it if I hadn't seen it for myself; they didn't exaggerate! Such wisdom and elegance—far more than I could ever have imagined."

1 Kings 10:1–9 MESSAGE

The queen herself was prompted to give gifts to Solomon: "She then gave the king four and a half tons of gold, and also sack after sack of spices and expensive gems. There hasn't been a cargo of spices like that since that shipload the queen of Sheba brought to King Solomon" (verse 10 MESSAGE). In fact, whole shiploads of treasure kept coming his way:

> The ships of Hiram also imported gold from Ophir along with tremendous loads of fragrant sandalwood and expensive gems. The king used the sandalwood for fine cabinetry in The Temple of GOD and the palace complex, and for making harps and dulcimers for the musicians. Nothing like that shipment of sandalwood has been seen since.

Verses 11–12 MESSAGE

Solomon even received twenty-five tons of gold in tribute annually, above and beyond the taxes and profit he made on trade with merchants and assorted kings and governors. He crafted two hundred shields of hammered gold, had a veneer of gold over his massive ivory throne, and had all his dinnerware made of pure gold. But gold was not his only treasure; he had a fleet of ocean-going ships and also imported horses and chariots from Egypt and exported them to all the kings of the Hittites and the kings of the Arameans (see 1 Kings 10:14–29; 2 Chronicles 1:14–17).

The Purpose of Prosperity

It is impossible to read the Bible with an open mind and miss the fact that "It is the blessing of the LORD that makes rich, and He adds no sorrow to it" (Proverbs 10:22). But some people would argue that this is an Old Testament revelation that does not apply to New Testament believers.

Do you really believe that an inferior covenant should provide superior benefits? Really? That might sound spiritual, but it actually is opposed to the Scriptures themselves. The writer of the book of Hebrews put it like this: "But now He [Jesus] has obtained a more excellent ministry, by as much as He is also the mediator of a better covenant, which has been enacted on better promises" (Hebrews 8:6).

God said the New Covenant is improved. It is a better covenant, and it provides superior promises. Why not embrace His promise and make the journey from the wilderness, the land of just enough, to the Promised Land, the land flowing with milk and honey, the land of more than enough? Why not reject poverty thinking, build a franchise with God and embrace His vision for your fantastic future?

Powerful Prayers

One evening after midnight in March 2016, Kathy and I were lying in bed, talking about our family. Seventeen years earlier, the Lord had instructed us to quit our ministry and build a legacy. In other words, I needed to stop doing ministry that did not have the generations to come in mind. He reminded us, "A good man leaves an inheritance to his children's children" (Proverbs 13:22). At the time we did not have much money, but we decided to open up a trust account for each of our seven grandkids (now we have eight) and put $50 a month in their accounts. As we lay there talking deep into the night, we recounted our divine mandate to affect the generations that would come after us. We wanted to do our part to build a wealth foundation to launch every member of our family into his or her God-given purpose.

So before we dozed off to sleep for the night, I said to Kathy, "Wouldn't it be great if God paid off our house so we could do more for our family?" (We had already been doubling up on our house payments for a couple of years to pay off our house early.) She agreed, so we held hands and prayed a simple prayer that God would pay off our house.

Six weeks later, Kathy and I were speaking at a conference in Southern California. After my last session, I got down from the stage to minister to some people who had come to the front of the church for prayer. About thirty people lined up in front of me, and I ministered to each one individually. Nearly an hour passed before I finally looked up and noticed that there was just one guy left in line. I motioned for him to come close and asked him what he needed prayer for.

"I didn't come here for prayer," he answered. "I've come here to pay off your house!"

I must have acted a little surprised, because he looked at me and continued, "You don't think I have the money, do you?"

"I have no idea," I responded, trying to understand his motive.

He pulled a large piece of paper out of his pants pocket and pointed to it. "Look, I have a purchase agreement for a boat for $600,000 that I'm buying this week! See," he insisted, "I have the money."

"I owe a lot of money on my house," I responded in unbelief.

"You don't owe more than three million dollars, do you? Because I have three million in the bank," he challenged.

"No! I owe about $500,000," I said sheepishly.

"Oh, that's a lot less than I thought you owed, so I just saved a bunch of money already."

"Listen, if you want to pay off my house, I need you to go talk to your pastor and tell him what you want to do. If he thinks it's a great idea, then we'll talk about it," I counseled.

"I already talked to God. He told me I should pay off your house! I want to do what He asked of me," he proclaimed.

"Well, it's my house, and I'm not good with you doing that unless you get some outside input into this word you have from the Lord," I said. Fearing I was going to be owned by this guy, I added, "Furthermore, if you do pay off my house, I don't want to be obligated to you for the rest of my life!"

"Kris, I just want to do what God asked me to do, and then I'm going to buy myself a boat. That's my only motive!" he assured me.

He texted me several more times over the next couple of days, urging me to let him pay off our house. On the fourth day, Kathy and I finally agreed to give him our bank information. The next day he paid our house off in full—$466,000! Three days later, he sent me a picture of a beautiful boat. The text read, "God said now that I've paid off your house, I can have any boat I want! So I got a much nicer boat than I was going to buy the first time."

This amazing guy changed my family's history with his generosity. I like the way he puts it: "I slayed your giant for you!" Yes, he did, and I'm so thankful to him for investing in my life.

This Gospel Doesn't Work Everywhere?

I began teaching on the subject of wealth a year before that generous guy paid off our house. The Lord told me that He wanted to take His people out of poverty and into prosperity. When I started teaching these principles, some people told me that I was preaching a gospel that would not work in Africa or among the poor. The fact is, the Gospel works everywhere. It is true that the application looks different in developing nations, but the mindsets are still the same.

It is also important to realize that, as John Adams so beautifully pointed out, the application of revelation is progressive. We see this in the life of Abraham and Sarah, who left their homeland not knowing where they were going, but knowing where they could not stay. They were literally poor wanderers when they set out on their journey. But as I shared earlier, God blessed them and they prospered. Each generation after Abraham grew in wealth and prosperity, until Abraham's grandson, Jacob/Israel, actually became a great nation. The progression of wealth continued to grow in the generations that followed, climaxing with King David and King Solomon.

Abraham's wealth would not have compared to Solomon's, but then again, wealth is first a condition of the soul, while the manifestations of wealth are relative to one's culture. Simply put, wealth in a village in Kenya is going to look different than wealth in the San Francisco Bay Area. Although the anointing is the same, the application will often look quite different. I have worked among the extreme poor of Africa for seventeen years. I am currently part of three orphanages, two in Mozambique and one in Kenya. We have also planted twelve ministry schools in eight African countries. Africa is the richest continent in the world with reference to natural resources, and the poorest continent in the world in terms of living conditions. I can tell you firsthand that Africa's main problem is not money; it is mindsets. The people who need this teaching the most are not middle-class Americans or Europeans; they are the poor of the world. We are teaching these principles in our schools in Africa because this is the Gospel, and the Gospel is relative to everyone, everywhere.

How about you, right where you are? I want my life to say to everyone, "Anything is possible." I want people who visit our house to think, "Everything is probable." I did not tell you our house story to brag, but to get your hopes up! "The testimony of Jesus is the spirit of prophecy" (Revelation 19:10). If God did this for us, then He will do it for you.

7

The Mindset of the Wealthy

Elon Musk sat on the L.A. freeway in bumper-to-bumper traffic, frustrated by "this enormous waste of time." As he pondered his situation, he began to dream of ways to solve the transportation dilemma that had plagued Southern Californians for seemingly forever. He began to envision a maze of "Hyperloop" tunnels bored at various levels underneath the city of Los Angeles, which would connect people to their ultimate destination. A few years later, through much red tape, near-miraculous inventions, and at the estimated cost of billions of dollars, Musk is now boring his first tunnels under his SpaceX parking lot. If successful, this Hyperloop transportation system will become a true superhighway that literally will put our cars on a roller skate and thrust us through the earth's surface at 120 miles per hour.

"Crazy!" you say.

This is just one of Musk's more insignificant endeavors. This guy wants to colonize Mars (yes, the planet Mars), making humanity a multiplanetary species by the year 2040.

"Daydreamer!" you say.

Maybe so, but he has already invented and built the most powerful rocket ever created in the history of the world. And oh, by the way, the rocket is reusable.

Elon Musk is rich, but he does not think big because he is rich; he got rich because he thinks big. Musk does not believe in God, but he does believe in doing the impossible.

I am baffled by the fact that the greatest thinkers in the world are often godless, humanistic, self-centered, self-absorbed atheists. This is an open indictment against the Body of Christ. It troubles me that many people who claim they are Christians live with limited, powerless, finite thinking. How is this even possible? How do people who claim to have the Creator of the universe living inside them, the mind of Christ thinking through them and the Spirit of God influencing the world around them even have the nerve to think small?

I propose that we believers don't have permission to live with limited mindsets. Consider the following distinct advantages of born-again believers.

1. We are the temple of the Holy Spirit.

Consequently, the God who envisioned everything and spoke the world(s) into existence lives inside us. Maybe we should all wear one of those signs on our chest that reads *God on Board*, just to remind ourselves of the fantastic cargo we carry (see 1 Corinthians 6:19).

2. We have access to the gift of wisdom.

The gift of wisdom is one of the nine supernatural gifts of the Holy Spirit listed in the book of 1 Corinthians. Think of it as the wisdom of King Solomon on steroids (see 1 Corinthians 12:8).

3. We have the mind of Christ, which means we think like God.

This one is otherworldly! We are God's divine think tank. Yet I have heard so many preachers misquote the Scripture on the mind of Christ that it drives me nuts. They often take the verses that teach us what we have in Christ and use them to *reduce* what God has meant to *inspire* us. Let's examine the verses together:

Yet we do speak wisdom among those who are mature; a wisdom, however, not of this age nor of the rulers of this age, who are passing away; but we speak God's wisdom in a mystery, the hidden wisdom which God predestined before the ages to our glory; the wisdom which none of the rulers of this age has understood; for if they had understood it they would not have crucified the Lord of glory; but just as it is written,

"*Things which eye has not seen and ear has not heard,*
And which have not entered the heart of man,
All that God has prepared for those who love him."

For to us God revealed them through the Spirit; for the Spirit searches all things, even the depths of God. For who among men knows the thoughts of a man except the spirit of the man which is in him? Even so the thoughts of God no one knows except the Spirit of God. Now we have received, not the spirit of the world, but the Spirit who is from God, so that we may know the things freely given to us by God, which things we also speak, not in words taught by human wisdom, but in those taught by the Spirit, combining spiritual thoughts with spiritual words.

But a natural man does not accept the things of the Spirit of God, for they are foolishness to him; and he cannot understand them, because they are spiritually appraised. But he who is spiritual appraises all things, yet he himself is appraised by no one. For *who has known the mind of the Lord, that he will instruct him?* But we have the mind of Christ.

1 Corinthians 2:6–16, emphasis added

The words in italics are statements made by an Old Testament prophet who was asking the question, "Who can understand what God is thinking about us?" Remember, the Old Testament people were not born again and did not have the Holy Spirit living inside them. They did not therefore have access to God's thoughts. But the apostle Paul points out in these verses that what was a mystery to them is actually revealed to us because we think like God. Read it for yourselves: We have received the Spirit of God, who knows the mind of God. Since the same Spirit lives in us who lived/lives in Jesus, we actually think like God. Do you want to know what God is thinking? What are *you* thinking? When you are right with God, you think His thoughts. The Old Testament prophet went on to ask, "Who has known the mind of the Lord . . . ?" In effect, the great apostle Paul replied, "We do! We have the mind of Christ."

The mind of Christ is your x factor, your secret weapon . . . your brain trust turbocharger. But to activate your heavenly advantage, you must lose the compliant, religious rule keeper, black-and-white mindset so you can journey out into the world of mystery, miracles and divine mayhem. We have become predictable, boring, vanilla, uninspired people. Yet our Founder is a radical, forethinking activist who, in three short years, altered the course of human history. Jesus transformed the way the world viewed God, money, nature, religion and Kingdom life.

4. We are a "new creation" born again into the Kingdom of God.

"Therefore, if anyone is in Christ, he is a new creation; old things have passed away; behold, all things have become new" (2 Corinthians 5:17 NKJV). The word *new* here means "prototype"—something never before created. Jesus said that John the Baptist was the greatest prophet of the entire Old Testament, but He went on to explain that the least in the Kingdom is greater than John (see Matthew 11:8–11). Consider some of the saints who lived in the Old Testament: Abraham, Moses, Elijah, Elisha, Esther, Deborah, David, Solomon and even Daniel. Daniel is a great example of the point I am making. He was ten times wiser than all the wise men of Babylon, yet we are greater than Daniel because we are new creatures in Christ. We are the first creatures to live on earth and in heaven simultaneously. Our head is not stuck in the clouds; it is positioned in heavenly places. Some people might think, *These guys are so heavenly minded that they're no earthly good.* But the truth is that we are so heavenly minded that we are full of earthly goods.

5. We are endowed with "the manifold wisdom of God."

By His "manifold wisdom," God reveals the mysteries of the Kingdom "through the church to the rulers and the authorities in the heavenly places" (Ephesians 3:10). The Greek word translated *manifold* here means "multicolored or multidimensional." Jesus has granted us multidimensional wisdom . . . the ability to understand challenging situations from every conceivable perspective and from every imaginable realm (see Ephesians 3:1–10).

6. We are seated in heavenly places with Christ.

This actually gives us another profound advantage. Think about it like this: Jesus told the apostle John, "Come up here, and I will show you what must take place after these things" (Revelation 4:1). In other words, our heavenly seat gives us insight into the future. There are so many ramifications to our raptured status (our position seated with Him in the heavenlies) that it makes my brain explode with possibility. For instance, what would happen if we could peer hundreds of years into the future and see the world the way it will be?

Maybe it is easier to illustrate by thinking of what it would be like if we lived in 1850 and were invited to "come up here" for a look at the world of 2017. In this exalted position, we would see televisions, computers, cars and planes, etc. . . . . a world much different from our own. What an amazing advantage this would give us as business people or inventors. Or how about if, in 1810, we were invited to view the future of medicine? We would see the diseases like polio, smallpox, tuberculosis and leprosy (to name a just a few) that plagued our generation be completely eradicated in the future.

This is not just a pipe dream or science fiction; this is our reality . . . our advantage . . . our right of passage . . . our inheritance as sons and daughters of the King.

7. Friendship with God is a game changer for us.

Jesus put it like this: "No longer do I call you slaves, for the slave does not know what his master is doing; but I have called you friends, for all things that I have heard from My Father I have made known to you" (John 15:15). When we transition from slavery to friendship with God (by keeping His commandments), suddenly we are introduced into a realm of revelation that only Jesus walked in. We have access to "all things" that were revealed to Jesus. Think of this level of supernatural revelation as *Google God*.

We followers of Jesus have many other profound advantages over those who have yet to experience His transforming power. But it should suffice to say that the most creative, inventive, ingenious, imaginative, inspired, brilliant, resourceful, innovative, advanced ideas should be flowing from the sons and daughters of God. When the believers in the first-century Corinthian church were struggling with jealousy and strife, the apostle Paul rebuked them by reminding them that they were behaving like "mere men" (see 1 Corinthians 3:3). We are not mere humans; we are alive in the Spirit. We are sons and daughters of the God of the universe. He endows us with wisdom, commissions us with power, and gives us the authority to make a profound difference in the world. It is past time that we rise to our high call in Christ Jesus and start thinking like royalty.

Stay Thirsty, My Friend

One of the main reasons believers get relegated to spectators in the game of creativity is that our brain gears get all mucked up with complacency. Complacency is to the mind what cancer is to the body. It seeps into the hearts of people and slowly anesthetizes its victims, until it finally chokes the hope out of people.

Consider the example of two of the greatest retailers of our time, Sears and Montgomery Ward. They were the first department stores in the history of America to market their wares through catalogs. Both corporations strategically placed catalog stores throughout the United States and connected them with huge, centrally located distribution centers that maximized their gigantic inventories. This was very cutting-edge thinking back in the day.

Why didn't these great, forward-thinking corporations with millions of dollars in inventory and massive purchasing discounts from a world of suppliers become the first Amazon or eBay? Why did these huge, world-class retail companies ever let Amazon or eBay even get started, much less get a leg up on them? (As of this writing, Montgomery Ward is gone and Sears is nearly bankrupt.) The simple answer is that they stopped dreaming and taking risks. Instead, they settled into the comfortable, slow death zone. The innovation that marked these great companies a century ago was replaced with complacent, lackluster attitudes and lethargic thinking. By the time they woke up, the Amazon monster had clawed its way out of the lagoon and had consumed everything in its path.

Religion has a way of fueling complacency in our lives. Religion anesthetizes our brains as it slowly seeps into our souls like a thick, black tar gumming up the gears of our imagination, until our innovative thinking finally grinds to a complete halt. To make matters worse, religious people are often the greatest resistors of new ideas and possibility thinking. When believers finally dare to leave the beaten path of limited thinking, they are often branded as heretics or cult leaders. The fact is, many Christians have more faith in the devil's ability to deceive us than in the Holy Spirit's ability to lead us into "all truth." We must admit that thinking is risky business. Mindlessness, however, is sure death!

A Hopeless Future

When the TED Talks moderator asked Elon Musk *why* he wanted to colonize Mars, Musk said, "I want to get up every morning with a hope for the future!"

To give people a hopeful future, this guy is building rockets to transport humans where they can inhabit a distant planet. In a sense, Musk is preaching our message! We have been commissioned to preach the Gospel, and the Gospel means Good News. Jesus put it like this: "The thief comes only to steal and kill and destroy; I came that they may have life, and have it abundantly" (John 10:10).

Consider this: When the children of Israel were led into captivity for seventy years in Babylon, the great prophet Jeremiah prophesied, "'For I know the plans that I have for you,' declares the LORD, 'plans for welfare and not for calamity to give you a future and a hope'" (Jeremiah 29:11). Hope for the future is the essential element to accessing unlimited thinking. In other words, in order to tap into eternal thinking, we must believe there is supposed to be a future. Why would anyone waste time thinking of divine solutions for world problems if there is not supposed to be a future? It is impossible to inspire people to straighten chairs on the deck of the sinking *Titanic*. It all just seems so futile to them.

I talk more about this subject in my book *Heavy Rain*. Here is a short excerpt from the chapter titled "It's a Wonderful World":

> In 1967, Louis Armstrong, an African American basking in the fresh flame of the civil rights movement, stared down the doomsayers of his era when he sang the famous song "What a Wonderful World." In the song, he sang about trees of green, and red roses, too, blooming "for me and you," and he thought to himself about "what a wonderful world" it is.[1] A couple of years ago, I downloaded the song onto my iPod and happened to listen to it for the first time during a flight on my way to a conference. The song unearthed a crisis in my soul, one so deep that I was unaware it even existed. As the song played, I found myself in a battle that is impossible to explain accurately with mere words, but I will try. My heart wrenched with every line of the lyrics as my mind engaged in a heated conflict within itself. My brain became a battlefield, and various Scriptures emerged as soldiers warring against one another in a kind of noble struggle for truth.
>
> I kept pushing replay on my iPod, because it felt as though Louis's words were reinforcements in my war for reality. As the hours passed, I came to understand that a foreboding spirit (foreboding means an impending sense of doom) had somehow lodged itself in my soul and was dictating my worldview. I realized that there was some sort of warped need in me to believe that things were getting worse in the world.[2]

I call this the Rapture syndrome. Our eschatology has become our kryptonite! Instead of the coming of the Lord bringing us a blessed hope, it has become our woeful future. Allow me to illustrate this with another example from the archives of *Heavy Rain*:

> I was born January 31, 1955, the same year that Steve Jobs and Bill Gates were born. And Bill Joy [the father of the Internet] was born in November 1954. These men were some of the main catalysts who birthed the Information Age. Few, if any, of the people who ushered in the Information Age were followers of Jesus Christ. Steve Jobs was a Buddhist, Bill Gates is an agnostic, Michael Dell is Jewish, and I am not sure about Bill Joy.
>
> . . . Have you ever wondered why there was hardly a single Christian at the forefront of the emerging Information Age? I believe it is because the Jesus movement, which largely embraced the *Late Great* eschatology, was birthed at the same time. Christian young people were all waiting for the great escape, leaving their non-Christian peers to follow the *kairos* clock of the Information Age and become the forerunners of the new epoch season. There were no Christian forerunners because there were no forethinkers. We were all taught to live for eternity, but no one seemed to understand that we were also supposed to live *from* eternity.[3]

Flipping the Switch

If we are going to embrace the mindset of wealth, where nothing is impossible to those who believe, we must ditch a life of complacency and embrace a hopeful future. Solomon said, "Hope deferred makes the heart sick, but desire fulfilled is a tree of life" (Proverbs 13:12). It is not when the thing I hope for gets deferred that it makes my heart sick; it is when *hope itself gets deferred*.

In other words, when I stop hoping, I am relegated to the dark night of the soul. Yet from the beginning of time, we were instructed by our heavenly Father to eat from the Tree of Life in the Garden of

Eden. The fruit of the Life tree is a *desire fulfilled*; it is not a long-ing delayed.

In the sixties, there was a slogan that promoted the use of LSD among young people: "Turn on, tune in and drop out!" Most believ-ers did not take acid, but they did "tune in" (to God) and "drop out" (of society). The catch-phrase of my generation was "last one out turn off the lights." We effectively relegated the world to a darkened understanding and consequently left behind the blind to lead the blind. Now it is time to arise and shine. We are the light of the world (not the light of the Church). Like Joseph in the days of Pharaoh, we are commissioned to bring heavenly solutions to earthly situa-tions. And like Joseph, whenever we touch the world, we bring with us the wealth of our Father's Kingdom, the abundant life of His divine providence, and His supernatural ability to do the impossible in every situation.

8

The Outrageously Artistic Nature
of God

In 1998 we were living in a small yellow cottage with a large covered porch; it was an old place surrounded by a white picket fence. Our bedroom window peered out into a flower garden that stretched the length of our home. One Saturday morning in the spring, I woke up at dawn in time to see the sun rise over the eastern sky, reflecting off the billowing clouds in the heavens. The rays of the sun painted the sky with breathtaking streaks of various shades of orange and red, which backlit the rolling, curling clouds, causing them to shimmer against the deep-blue heavens. This created a canopy of bliss moving slowly in a sort of silent rhythm. The garden's flowers stretched upward into the window, filling the entire frame with a living display of blossoms of infinite shapes. Radiant yellow nuclei surrounded by deep purple petals, scattered within an endless paradise of countless other blossoms, moved softly in the gentle spring breeze.

I stared out the window for what seem like an eternity in a kind of ecstasy, as my soul grappled to comprehend the sheer grandeur of the vast expanse spread out before me. My mind was swirling with awe!

Suddenly, the voice of God transcended my raptured state. *Do you know why I created flowers?* He inquired.

I was not sure if I should guess until I exhausted my intellect, or just posture my soul to receive a massive revelation. I wondered if the Lord was going to unleash for me the mystery of His creation, which had likely been locked up in the vaults of heaven for eons of ages past. I recalled His conversation with George Washington Carver, when He gave him the astonishing, unfolding revelation of the peanut, which became the foundation for several patents. Then I quickly seized on Ezekiel's experience in the valley of dry bones, when God asked him a ridiculous question: "Can these bones live?" The great prophet, in a similar situation to mine, did not want to sound unbelieving. Yet he also knew he must not lie to his Master, so he blurted out, "O Lord God, You know" (Ezekiel 37:3).

Hastily, I decided to plead ignorance and see what transpired, so I sheepishly said, *I have no idea.*

I think they're pretty! He replied.

I lay there thinking, *And . . . ? Seriously, is that it? You think they're pretty? No heavy revelations? No deep insights into the ecosystems of the cosmos? No third heaven, come-up-here kind of experience? That's it?*

I lay there awhile longer, hoping my patience would inspire God to go on. But no, nothing else . . . no voice . . . no vision . . . no revelation . . . no insights . . . just *I think they're pretty!*

Months later, I happened upon a statement that Jesus made, and suddenly a whole new side of the nature of God exploded within me. Jesus said,

Consider the lilies, how they grow: they neither toil nor spin; but I tell you, not even Solomon in all his glory clothed himself like one of these. But if God so clothes the grass in the field, which is alive today and tomorrow is thrown into the furnace, how much more will He clothe you? You men of little faith!

Luke 12:27–28

The lilies don't toil or spin, yet in spite of the fact that they don't work and they don't provide a ton of benefit, God still made them beautiful. In other words, God likes cool stuff. God loves art. He values beauty, even if it does not last long or has no other advantage.

By now you might be saying, "What does this have to do with wealth, or with anything, for that matter?"

It has everything to do with wealth. Let me take you on a short historic journey that highlights the incredible revelation of the nature of God. In the absence of the printing press, and with the scarcity of the Scriptures and the illiteracy of the congregation, it was bestowed on the fathers of the early Church to create a cultural experience that emulated the nature of God. These church fathers were steeped in the revelation of the splendor, majesty and glory of the Lord, and they needed a way to communicate in the congregational gatherings the sheer nature of His greatness and divinity.

Of course, this all predated videos, movies and the inventions and innovations of the modern world. So from about the third century on, the early Church began building monasteries and cathedrals that would capture the greatness, splendor, majesty, grandeur and glory of God. Subsequently, majestic stone walls were erected, gracing the skies with transcendent beauty. Stained-glass windows traversed across the sanctuary, whispering the Gospel story in majestic rays of light. Polished marble floors glistening in the morning sun reflected the King's magnificence. Podiums elevated to midheaven facilitated the thunderous voice of the priesthood. And all this was designed as a multidimensional learning experience where the parishioners participated in the discovery of the nature of our outrageously artistic God.

But much like the outlandishly expensive perfume Mary poured over the body of Christ, and the subsequent tongue-lashing she endured from His disciples about how it was a waste and how the perfume could have been sold and the money given to the poor, we Protestants have scorned the majestic display of the Gospel in the name of stewardship. Unknowingly, we have stripped the Good News of its beauty, embracing a colorless, drab, monochrome message absent of majesty and groping for divinity. Gone are the regal church bells ringing from the lovely steeples, echoing the hymns of our Savior, waking the city and beckoning them to gather to Him. The bells have been replaced by video announcements or a PowerPoint display, which pale in sheer grandeur and magnificence.

Gone is the splendor of hand-carved walls and statues of angels. They have been supplanted by warehouses and storefront structures, as if heaven were paved with asphalt streets and entered through metal doors instead of pearly gates.

Gone are citadels with their priceless paintings, painstakingly brushed on their skyward ceilings by famous artists. They have been swapped out for dropped ceilings and white tiles.

Gone are the majestic, stained-glass windows breathlessly reaching from floor to the ceiling, filling the onlooker with the awareness of the Limitless One. In their place stand Sheetrocked walls, monotonous textures and drab decor.

Lost in the display of splendor is the revelation of the very nature of God—His omniscience, His omnipresence and His supernatural power. In our zeal to be frugal stewards of our finite resources, we have exchanged the nature of our majestic King for that of a suffering servant. Yet the apostle John reminded us that "as He is, so also are we in this world" (1 John 4:17). John did not say "as He was," but "as He is." Although Jesus will forever be the Lamb of God, He is now revealed as the coming King, who sits at the right hand of the Father and rules the world with a rod of iron. In other words, Jesus has elevated us with Him to the third heaven and has seated us with Him on His throne. Our heavenly mandate is to make earth like heaven.

Spirit-Filled Craftsman

By now you might be thinking that all these stained-glass windows and beautiful buildings feel carnal and worldly. Let me challenge the very idea of what is and is not spiritual by taking you way back to the days of Moses. God instructed Moses to build Him the Tabernacle, and He gave Moses comprehensive instructions for it, right down to the smallest detail. The Tabernacle of Moses, as God called it, was to be incredibly beautiful, with hand-carved statues and pillars, lots of brightly colored materials and loads of gold, silver and bronze. In fact, Moses's Tabernacle was to be so complex and so ornate that one of Moses's greatest challenges was finding skilled people who could actually build it. After all, the entire Israelite population was made up of former slaves who had had little opportunity to engage in creativity. Yet true to His nature, God had an answer. Look at the exchange God had with Moses about it:

> Now the LORD spoke to Moses, saying, "See, I have called by name Bezalel, the son of Uri, the son of Hur, of the tribe of Judah. I have filled him with the Spirit of God in wisdom, in understanding, in knowledge, and in all kinds of craftsmanship, to make artistic designs for work in gold, in silver, and in bronze, and in the cutting of

stones for settings, and in the carving of wood, that he may work in all kinds of craftsmanship."

Exodus 31:1–5

Bezalel was the very first person ever mentioned in the Bible as being filled with the Holy Spirit. Like Jesus, he was filled with the Spirit, but for a distinct yet different purpose than our Lord. Remember, Isaiah tells us that Jesus was filled with the Spirit specifically to preach the Good News, bind up the brokenhearted, release captives and free prisoners (see Isaiah 61:1–4). But the Spirit filled Bezalel for a completely different reason. Bezalel was not releasing captives or freeing prisoners; instead, the Spirit of God within him gave him the supernatural ability for creativity. God anointed him to cut stones, carve wood and create beautiful things with gold, silver and bronze. To Bezalel, artistry was spiritual!

Warning, Warning . . . Warning?

The apostle John warned us about "the lust of the flesh and the lust of the eyes and the boastful pride of life" (1 John 2:16). Sometimes when we read verses like this, we can walk away feeling as though beautiful things are just evil temptations that godly people should avoid. But the truth is that beauty was God's idea. It therefore has to be inherently good, because it is a reflection of His impeccable nature and flawless character.

Lust is not inherent in the object of its desire. Most often, it is a condition in the heart of the onlookers. The question is not, What do you like? The question is, What do you treasure? When you treasure earthly things and have little or no value for heavenly things, you exchange the Blesser for the blessing and relegate your passion to perversion . . . the wrong version. But appreciating beauty in itself is not wrong. It is undeniable that God appreciates beauty. He comments more than thirty times on the beauty of several different women throughout the Bible. He calls Abraham's Sarah beautiful and Isaac's Rebekah stunning. And Jacob fell in love with Rachel, whom the Bible says "was beautiful of form and face" (Genesis 29:17). Esther was gorgeous, and so was Abigail, one of David's many wives. And who can forget the beauty of Bathsheba or of Absalom's sister, Tamar?

God is the Ultimate Artist, the Master Painter and the Magnificent Sculptor. He loves beauty, He created the concept of splendor, and He lives in glory. The great apostle Paul put it best: "For since the creation of the world His invisible attributes, His eternal power and divine nature, have been clearly seen, being understood through what has been made" (Romans 1:20). In other words, the very nature of God is on display in creation. Creation is God's reality show, His classroom and His university. Yet it seems as though many of us often cut His classes or are absent from His divine lectures.

I want to challenge you to slow down, smell the roses, walk among the Redwood trees, climb a mountain or just chillax at the beach while you allow the warm summer sand to seep through your toes. Go ahead and muse on the wealth and utter grandeur of God. This is God's world—His heavenly theater—so make sure you don't miss the movie!

PART TWO

Practical Ways to Grow Your Capacity for Wealth

In the second part of this book, I will help you discover some practical ways to increase your personal capacity for wealth. I will also show you some hands-on skills that you can use in your everyday life. I hope these things will help you prosper both in your ability to lead others and in your aptitude for growing in competence and confidence.

9

The Tyranny of the Glass Jar

In the summer of 1985, Kathy and I opened our first auto parts store in Weaverville, California. With a name like Weaverville, it is probably obvious that it was a small town. At the time we already owned two auto repair shops and a service station, so it felt like the logical next step in the growth of our business. But more importantly, the Lord actually instructed me to open an auto parts store. We called our store Crossroad Auto Parts. Our motto was "Excellent service, the Crossroad difference" because we were determined to serve the automotive needs of our community in a way that no one had ever experienced before.

When we launched our new endeavor, there were already three other auto parts stores in our tiny community of approximately three thousand people. By 1988, two of the other stores had crashed and burned, leaving us with just one massive competitor. It was a NAPA store owned by a medium-sized corporation, which had about fifteen other stores in California. In spite of our tough competitor, we grew rapidly for the first four years, and then our sales began to level off at around $600,000 annually. Over the next two years after that, our sales remained pretty much flat.

By year six I started to wrestle with the lack of growth in our business, because I believe that healthy things grow. I asked myself several questions that led us to a process of discovery. One of the questions that intrigued me the most was, *We are an auto parts supplier, so why can I predict within a few hundred dollars—a year before anyone's car breaks down—how many parts we will sell?* For example, why is the number of fan belts we will sell next August already predetermined twelve months before anyone's fan belt fails? As I searched for answers, I discovered through an inquiry that the NAPA store's sales were also predictable. *Why*, I wondered, *do the sales of each of our stores feel predetermined?* Another question that challenged me was, *Why did we grow so fast, experiencing double-digit increases every year, and then suddenly stop growing?*

I soon discovered that the simple answer to these questions was *capacity*. Webster defines *capacity* as "the potential or suitability for holding, storing or accommodating." With this in mind, I envisioned our auto parts store as a large glass jar, and I pictured our customers as water being poured into the jar. Of course, the jar offers virtually no restriction or constraint until it reaches full capacity. But once it is full, it cannot contain any more water, no matter how fast or slow I pour. If I introduce pressure and force fresh water into the jar, the stale water will spill out to make room for the fresh water. No matter what I do to modify the water's delivery system (i.e., a larger hose, more water pressure, etc.), the jar's capacity is predetermined and is therefore unaffected by a higher volume of water. In other words, Crossroad Auto Parts was a glass jar, and there were invisible walls around our store that predetermined our capacity or ability to take care of our customers. We were also *in* a glass jar, however—namely a small town, which helped determine our capacity.

I understand that this is Business 101, but we somehow missed this lesson about capacity in our first four businesses. So in response to my simple revelation, I gathered my team of twelve at my house and set up a large whiteboard. I drew a large jar on the board while our staff patiently looked on. Then I pointed to my picture of a glass jar and said, "This is the invisible jar that is called Crossroad Auto Parts. The water in the jar represents our customers, and the jar is full! Tell me what the invisible walls are, and how we can expand our capacity to serve more customers."

Our workers looked at me with a sort of stupid grin, as if to say, "We have no idea what you're talking about."

"Okay," I continued, "when customers get pressed up against the walls of the glass jar, they usually complain or never come back. What do our customers consistently complain about?"

The workers' faces lit up as if they finally got it, and they began talking over one another as they struggled to communicate our customers' complaints to me. One big complaint was, "Our phones are always busy, and our shop customers can't get through to us. They scream at us all the time about having to call back ten times before the phone finally rings!" Here is the list of the other four complaints our customers had about us:

1. We don't have enough depth on the fast-moving part numbers. We run out of the fast-moving parts every day, and then we have to send our customers to our competitor to get what they need.
2. We close at 5:00 p.m., but the local repair shops don't close until 6:00 p.m., so they go to NAPA after we close.
3. We only have two countermen on from noon to 2:00 p.m. to accommodate everyone's lunch break. These are two of the busiest hours of the day, so people walk out of the store because they get tired of waiting.

4. Henry is not a very good counterman, so the shop guys hang up and call our competitor when he answers the phone. (Yes, poor Henry was present to hear this; these guys could be brutally honest.)

The next day, I could hardly wait to get started increasing our capacity. Within a week, we tackled the big complaint and installed two more phone lines, designating those two lines as "wholesale lines." We took our two best countermen and assigned them to the wholesale phone lines so that the professional mechanics would not have to deal with Henry, our inexperienced counterman. We extended our hours until 6:00 p.m., and we also opened two hours earlier. I took a late lunch and manned the wholesale lines from noon to 2:00 p.m. with one other guy. This gave us better coverage during one of the busiest times of the day. Finally, we doubled the depth of our inventory on the top 20 percent of the most popular part numbers. (It is always embarrassing to run out of the parts that every customer assumes you should carry.) This also improved our reputation, and the outcome was stunning. That year, our business grew to $750,000 in sales. That was a 25 percent increase in one year!

Ideating became an ongoing exercise in our business culture because of the amazing impact it had on our bottom line. Twice a year we would gather at my house for pizza. Then I would set up the whiteboard and draw a jar, and the passionate dialogue would begin. After we did this a few times, our team members started keeping notes on their insights throughout the year so they could bring them to the discussion. This created a culture of highly productive conversations. The next year, we began giving bonuses to our employees when we used their suggestions, which fueled the fires of innovation and creativity.

An interesting thing happened through the evolution of our innovation: Every time we would improve one thing, that very innovation would *require* us to enhance or improve something else. One simple example I remember was the phone lines that we added to eliminate the constant busy signals. The extra lines had unexpected side effects. Suddenly, there was not enough staff on the counters to answer the calls, so we went from busy signals to customers waiting on hold. This led to several procedure improvements. For example, when a shop customer called, the counterman would get all the information (year, make, model, parts required), and then call the customer right back when he had a handle on the parts and availability. That way, the mechanics were not hanging on the phone for fifteen unproductive minutes, waiting for information. We also added more people on the counter and restructured their other duties to put them near the phones during high traffic times.

You might be asking yourself why I am giving you so many details. The reason is, I want you to understand that you can (almost) always grow your capacity in business and in life. If you are involved in an organization that serves people (a business, family, church, school, government, etc.), then I challenge you to use the whiteboard and jar exercise with yourself and your team.

Measuring Your Personal Capacity

Growing an organization's capacity can be exciting, but it is not nearly as fulfilling as increasing your personal capacity. In fact, if you grow your organization's capacity large enough, don't be surprised if you become the limiting factor, the greatest constraint, or the wall of glass that is undermining the extraordinary growth in the life of your organization. It is therefore extremely important for you to grow your personal capacity as you grow the capacity of the organizations you lead.

Measuring your personal capacity is a little more complicated than measuring business capacity, because there are no sales reports or profit and loss statements. To make things even more complex, there are also many different types of personal capacity. Growth in one dimension of your life does not necessarily guarantee growth anywhere else. How can you tell when your personal "jar" is full? If flat sales are an indication in the business world that a firm is at full capacity, what are the equivalent signs in your personal life?

Unfortunately, I think people often discover they are at full capacity when they stop being fully functional, or when they crash in some area of their lives. They extend themselves beyond their capacity, and they suffer the side effects of being overextended. I had this exact experience in 2008 and ended up on the couch for six months, completely unable to function. It all began when one of my close family members had a serious nervous breakdown. This person could not come out of the bedroom for months, which of course had a terrible effect on the rest of the family.

In the midst of that horrible situation, my son, who is a pastor on our staff and who also has three little children, found out that his marriage was over. As if all that were not bad enough, in that same month Bill Johnson was diagnosed with hepatitis A, which laid him up for six weeks. Consequently, I was tasked with trying to cover several of his speaking engagements (plus my own) in four different countries.

It was the perfect storm—perfectly bad, that is—for an overly responsible person like me. I knew I was beyond my soul's capacity to cope with this much pain, because I started experiencing high levels of anxiety that taxed my mind and body like a plague. I felt trapped by the impossible circumstances that seemed to worsen by the day. As the days turned into months, on top of my intense anxiety I began experiencing severe depression that literally paralyzed me for weeks. It took me a year to recover and another year to find a new, healthy rhythm in my life.

One of the things I learned in that horrible season is that pain of some sort is often the first indicator that our capacity is over-extended. Pain is like the idiot light on the dashboard of our car, which indicates that something is malfunctioning. Let me give you a real-life example. The other day, a young man picked me up from an airport in a foreign country. While we were driving, I noticed a piece of black tape on the instrument panel of his car, so I asked, "What's that black tape doing on your dashboard?"

"Oh," he explained, "there's a light flashing on my dash and I can't afford to get it fixed right now, so I put a piece of tape over it so it doesn't drive me nuts."

"Drive you nuts! Pretty soon it's not going to drive you at all," I teased.

I have to admit that in my terrible season, I was just like my foreign friend. The trouble light was flashing on the dashboard of my life, but I just covered it up with a hundred reasons why I could not stop and fix it. Finally, my soul, mind and body just shut down completely, leaving me to die on the highway of self-importance.

Growing Vines and Pruning Sticks

Jesus told us a great but often misunderstood story about a vine and a vinedresser. He said, "I am the true vine, and My Father is the vine-dresser. Every branch in Me that does not bear fruit, He takes away; and every branch that bears fruit, He prunes it so that it may bear more fruit" (John 15:1–2). Jesus went on to say that we are the branches of the vine, and either we get pruned back or completely cut off.

This parable reminds me of my Uncle Sally, who had a small vineyard when I was a teenager. I used to work on his farm once in a while in the summer. This is where I learned about the organic dynamics of grapevines. Left unattended, a vine will spend all its energy extending its branches, until it literally has no energy left to produce leaves, much less fruit. For instance, if you find a branch twenty feet long, the first five feet will have grapes on it. The next three feet will only have leaves, and the last twelve feet of the same branch will be just one long stick. A grapevine simply becomes a stick tree if it gets overextended. If you don't prune the branch all the way back to its area of fruitfulness, then the vine's capacity to produce fruit will be siphoned off to grow sticks.

This is a great example of our own lives. If we overextend ourselves beyond our personal calling and don't prune (quit) our activities that are fruitless, we use the capacity we do have on things that don't really matter. Thus, we undermine our divine responsibility and derail our destiny.

Increasing Your Capacity

There were three things I learned from my dark night of the soul season. First, there are limits to what I can carry. If I violate those boundaries, I will become useless. Second, I am not the savior of the world. There is always enough capacity, however, for everything God has called me to accomplish. And third, if I don't assess my capacity and understand my limits, at some point I will probably blow up my life.

On the other hand, one of the exciting things I have learned over the years is that you can actually increase your personal capacity in the same way that I demonstrated in my Crossroad Auto Parts example. In fact, it is your ability to grow your capacity that causes you to become a truly wealthy person. I want to share a few ways that you can grow your capacity. These are just examples of some of the ways you can expand your capability, though there are hundreds more. The lessons I want to talk about are found in the story in Matthew 25:14–28, where Jesus told about a master who called his servants together and gave each of them a sum of money, *according to their ability*. I will quote this story more fully in the next chapter, but to summarize, the master gave the first servant five talents. A talent was worth about $30,000 in today's funds, so the first guy received approximately $150,000. The second servant received three talents, or $90,000, and the third received one talent, or $30,000. Again, the amount of money they received was directly related to their ability—or you could say to their capacity—to steward wealth.

Their master empowered these guys to steward his money while he was on a long journey. Later on, he returned and asked each of them to give an account of their stewardship. The first servant confidently replied (in my paraphrasing), "Master, I took your $150,000 and I doubled it, making you another $150,000!"

His master was so proud of him that he said, "Well done, good and faithful slave. You were faithful with a few things, I will put you in charge of many things; enter into the joy of your master" (Matthew 25:21).

The same thing happened with the second servant. He took his master's $60,000 and increased it to $120,000, doubling his master's investment. The master repeated the same exhortation to him: "Well done, good and faithful slave. You were faithful with a few things, I will put you in charge of many things; enter into the joy of your master" (verse 23).

The third servant was a completely different story. The guy was so afraid of failing that he took the master's $30,000 and buried it. This guy certainly was not the sharpest knife in the drawer! Listen to his excuse: "Master, I knew you to be a hard man, reaping where you did not sow and gathering where you scattered no seed. And I was afraid, and went away and hid your talent in the ground. See, you have what is yours" (verses 24–25).

Before we dialogue about the rest of this guy's stupidity, did you notice how he told his master that he knew the man expected to receive a return on his investment? That is like getting pulled over for speeding and telling the officer, "I knew that speeding was wrong, so I went faster." I mean, the guy was a knucklehead.

The master had no patience for his slave's outright rebellion. He replied, "You wicked, lazy slave, you knew that I reap where I did not sow and gather where I scattered no seed. Then you ought to have put my money in the bank, and on my arrival I would have received my money back with interest" (verses 26–27).

But wait, it gets worse for the guy. His master commanded, "Take away the talent from him, and give it to the one who has the ten talents" (verse 28). Yet it is the master's final exhortation that completely undoes me: "For to everyone who has, more shall be given, and he will have an abundance; but from the one who does not have, even what he does have shall be taken away" (verse 29). Here are five things we can learn from this story:

1. What you have been given monetarily is directly proportionate to your capacity to steward it.

Each of the servants was given money equal to his ability. In other words, your personal capacity determines the level of your wealth. There is an old axiom that says if you took all the money in the world and divided it up equally, five years later the rich would be rich again, the middle class would return to being the middle class, and the poor would become poor again. Of course, we have no way of knowing how accurate this axiom is. But one thing we do know for certain is that people who win a million dollars or more in the lottery are usually in worse financial shape five years later than before they won. This is a great example of the practical ramifications of the lack of personal capacity in a person's life. Most people who win the lottery become richer on the outside than the capacity for wealth that they carry within. This ultimately creates a lack of sustainability.

A similar dynamic is also commonplace when people receive a large inheritance without growing their personal capacity for wealth. Since they did not participate in the process of creating the wealth, they bypassed the progression of expanding their capacity as they increased their affluence. This usually results in one of two attitudes. Either they have no value for the money because they did not have to endure the sacrifices it took to make it, so they waste it all on stupid living. Or they fear losing the money because they have no idea how it was created, so this typically results in the "hoarding complex" in which they hide the money somewhere so that nobody in the family can use it and risk losing it. Doesn't this remind you of the guy with one talent?

2. If you are faithful, both your investment and your capacity for wealth will grow.

Two of the servants were faithful with what they had the capacity to handle, and after their financial success, they were given even more. If you are faithful with what you have been given and invest it wisely, not only will your investment grow, but you will also increase your personal capacity for wealth.

3. Risk expands our capacity for wealth; whatever you don't use, you lose!

The third servant hid his money out of his fear of failure. His master took the money away from him and gave it to the guy who already had the most money, *because* that man was the wisest and most faithful servant. Whatever you don't use, you lose!

Risk expands our capacity for wealth. Without risk, we atrophy in apathy or we wither in fear. In fact, Jesus called the servants who increased their wealth *faithful* and called the one who refused to take risks *lazy* and *wicked*. It is important to understand that it is not financial profit that increases our personal capacity; instead, it is faithfulness to work hard and invest wisely. We often cannot control the outcome of our labor. Consequently then, success in God is measured by faithfulness, hard work, wise stewardship and perseverance. The apostle James drives this point home when he warns us about being overconfident in our ability to produce a profit:

> Come now, you who say, "Today or tomorrow we will go to such and such a city, and spend a year there and engage in business and make a profit." Yet you do not know what your life will be like tomorrow. Instead, you ought to say, "If the Lord wills, we will live and also do this or that."

James 4:13–15

The Lord is ultimately the only one who can control the outcome of our efforts. Taking risks—in the Lord—is therefore actually partnering with God. Let me be clear: I am not talking about taking dumb risks for the sake of growing our capacity (or for any other reason, for that matter). I am saying that you can only grow in God if you take wise, prayerful risks that put your talents in the fire of faithfulness and hard work.

I doubt that most of us would see a person who refuses to invest or steward the resources God has given him or her as wicked (maybe as lazy, but not as wicked). It is right there in black and white, however.

The greatest Lover of all time called a hole-digging money hoarder *wicked*.

"Yikes, that's harsh," you complain.

True, but the urgency of Jesus' words awakens us to realize that He gives us good gifts to use for the benefit of others. The hole-digging spirit buries our potential and hides our possibilities in counterfeit security and photoshopped reality. It undermines the God-given need inbred in us for adventure, and it relegates us to a predictable existence in the land of the boring. That land is inhabited by the overinsured, riskless souls who long for the government to take care of them. Together they scream, "Tax the rich suckers! They owe us! We're victims of an unjust system! We should all be equal!"

Meanwhile, the invisible force of God continues to transfer wealth from the hands of the lazy, fearful people into the hands of the faithful, risk-taking stewards.

4. In the Kingdom, faithfulness is a sign of a wealthy soul and attracts money.

Oddly, we also learn that the Kingdom actually causes the wealthy to get wealthier and the poor to get poorer. Or maybe a better way to look at it is that faithfulness is a sign of a wealthy soul, which consequently attracts money. This creates a kind of wealth ecosystem that operates something like this: Everybody begins with attracting money according to his or her current ability or capacity. Those who are faithful and wise stewards take risks and invest the money. The Lord honors faithful risk and causes their money to grow. As the money grows, God blesses the people who were given stewardship of the money, and He increases their capacity to handle even more money . . . and the beat goes on.

5. People who look like "victims" or "gold fingers" are actually living out the financial ramifications of their own actions.

Some people who look like the victims of an unjust system are actually just casualties of their own inability to live up to their full capacity and be faithful stewards of what was entrusted to them. Others who seem to have a gold finger are actually just people who took calculated risks that led to incalculable reward.

We will explore more ways to increase our capacity for wealth in the remainder of this book. But it should suffice to say here that God has given each of us something to steward, something to invest, or a talent to grow for the sake of the Kingdom. It does not matter how little or how much you have; it is what you do with what you have been given that matters. So take some time to press against the glass walls of your capacity and begin to ask God for wisdom and insight into your constraints. Then develop a plan and muster the courage to increase your soul's capacity for more.

10

A Practical Look at Prosperity

Often when believers talk about wealth and prosperity, the conversations tend to focus on the philosophy and/or theology of the subject. This can lead us to believe that financial skills are either unnecessary or at least nonessential in the creation of wealth. I have discovered that although systemic poverty is complex, the lack of skill and understanding about how simple economies function is often one of the root causes of poverty. In this chapter I have therefore set out to lay a foundation around some simple, yet profound truths regarding the creation of wealth. I will also give you some practical skills that will help you grow in prosperity.

Let's begin by reviewing the mandate our Lord left with us. Jesus exhorted us to "make disciples of all the nations . . . teaching them to observe all that I commanded you" (Matthew 28:19–20). Five hundred years earlier, the great prophet Isaiah made a similar declaration, which climaxed in the most amazing outcome in the entire Bible concerning cultural reformation. He said that in the last days, "Many peoples will come and say, 'Come, let us go up to the mountain of the LORD, to the house of the God of Jacob; that He may

teach us concerning His ways and that we may walk in His paths'"
(Isaiah 2:3). What is amazing about Isaiah's prophecy is the outcome
of how the nations come to believers to learn the ways of the Lord:
"Nation will not lift up sword against nation, and never again will
they learn war"(verse 4).

The pressing question, then, is, what did Jesus teach us that would
be so profoundly powerful that it would cause the nations of the
world never to go to war with each other again? I am sure the answer is much more complex than the scope of this chapter, but I
believe that at least part of the answer involves the wisdom of God
surrounding our financial dealings—on both spiritual and practical levels. And on a practical level, a huge piece of the prosperity
puzzle lies in the contrast between the parable of the talents and the
parable of the minas.

A Tale of Two Parables

Let's step back into the parable of the talents, told in Matthew 25,
one more time and contrast it with the parable of the minas, told
in Luke 19, to unearth one of the most divine secrets of a wealth
culture for the nations. (Here is a hint: Read the two parables slowly,
looking for the distinctions between the two.)

The Parable of the Talents

For it [the kingdom of heaven] is just like a man about to go on a
journey, who called his own slaves and entrusted his possessions to
them. To one he gave five talents, to another, two, and to another,
one, each according to his own ability; and he went on his journey.
Immediately the one who had received the five talents went and traded
with them, and gained five more talents. In the same manner the
one who had received the two talents gained two more. But he who

received the one talent went away, and dug a hole in the ground and hid his master's money.

Now after a long time the master of those slaves came and settled accounts with them. The one who had received the five talents came up and brought five more talents, saying, "Master, you entrusted five talents to me. See, I have gained five more talents." His master said to him, "Well done, good and faithful slave. You were faithful with a few things, I will put you in charge of many things; enter into the joy of your master."

Also the one who had received the two talents came up and said, "Master, you entrusted two talents to me. See, I have gained two more talents." His master said to him, "Well done, good and faithful slave. You were faithful with a few things, I will put you in charge of many things; enter into the joy of your master."

And the one also who had received the one talent came up and said, "Master, I knew you to be a hard man, reaping where you did not sow and gathering where you scattered no seed. And I was afraid, and went away and hid your talent in the ground. See, you have what is yours."

But his master answered and said to him, "You wicked, lazy slave, you knew that I reap where I did not sow and gather where I scattered no seed. Then you ought to have put my money in the bank, and on my arrival I would have received my money back with interest. Therefore take away the talent from him, and give it to the one who has the ten talents."

Matthew 25:14–28

The Parable of the Minas

A nobleman went to a distant country to receive a kingdom for himself, and then return. And he called ten of his slaves, and gave them ten minas and said to them, "Do business with this until I come back." But his citizens hated him and sent a delegation after him, saying, "We do not want this man to reign over us." When he returned, after receiving the kingdom, he ordered that these slaves, to whom he had given the money, be called to him so that he might know what business they had done. The first appeared, saying, "Master, your mina has made ten minas more." And he said to him, "Well done, good slave, because you have been faithful in a very little thing, you are to be in authority over ten cities." The second came, saying, "Your mina, master, has made five minas." And he said to him also, "And you are to be over five cities." Another came, saying, "Master, here is your mina, which I kept put away in a handkerchief; for I was afraid of you, because you are an exacting man; you take up what you did not lay down and reap what you did not sow." He said to him, "By your own words I will judge you, you worthless slave. Did you know that I am an exacting man, taking up what I did not lay down and reaping what I did not sow? Then why did you not put my money in the bank, and having come, I would have collected it with interest?" Then he said to the bystanders, "Take the mina away from him and give it to the one who has the ten minas." And they said to him, "Master, he has ten minas already." I tell you that to everyone who has, more shall be given, but from the one who does not have, even what he does have shall be taken away.

Luke 19:12–26

One of the most amazing insights into the mind of God in the entire Bible lies hidden in these two simple parables. In fact, one of them contains the only clear strategy about how to make disciples of *cities* anywhere in Scripture. Did you catch the distinct contrasts that leap off the page when you compare the parables to one another? Here are three of the contrasts:

- In the parable of the talents, the slaves received money according to their ability.

- *In the parable of the minas, they were given about $500 each, and all of them received the same amount of money.*

- In the parable of the talents, the faithful slaves said to the master, "I have made you more talents."
- *In the parable of the minas, the faithful slaves said to the master, "Your minas have made more minas."*

- In the parable of the talents, the faithful slaves were rewarded by being put over many "things."
- *In the parable of the minas, the faithful slaves were given authority over "cities."*

The talent parable teaches us that God rewards hard work and faithfulness. But the parable of the minas shows us that the secret of having authority over cities lies in the ability to understand the power of wealth. In other words, when those faithful slaves said, "Master, your mina has made more minas," it means that they had figured out how money works for you instead of you working for money. The Lord basically said, "If you can figure out how to create a healthy ecosystem where money makes money, then you should have authority over cities." The connotation is that God is looking for people who are architects of a wealth culture to lead cities, because He wants cities to prosper.

We have a river, not a pond, within us. This means the power to make wealth must benefit the world around us, not lie stagnant in our soul. When God restores us, He gives us a mandate to use our own restoration to heal cities. This concept is captured in one of the most profound passages in the entire Bible:

The Spirit of the Lord GOD is upon me, because the LORD has anointed me to bring good news to the afflicted; He has sent me to bind up the brokenhearted, to proclaim liberty to captives and freedom to prisoners; to proclaim the favorable year of the LORD and the day of vengeance of our God; to comfort all who mourn, to grant those who mourn in Zion, giving them a garland instead of ashes, the oil of gladness instead of mourning, the mantle of praise instead of a spirit of fainting. So they will be called oaks of righteousness, the planting of the LORD, that He may be glorified. Then they will rebuild the ancient ruins, they will raise up the former devastations; *and they will repair ruined cities*, the desolations of many generations.

Isaiah 61:1–4, emphasis added

These verses teach us that when God heals us, we have a responsibility to take our personal restoration and extend it to our broken cities. Our personal victory is meant to benefit our communities. With that said, I would like to present to you a few very practical lessons about the creation of wealth and about money itself to both benefit you personally and to bless your city.

The Law of Fulfilled Expectations

The secret of McDonald's success is not in their sauce or even in their fries. It is actually in their system. To demonstrate my point, let me ask you a question. Can you make a better hamburger than McDonald's? Most people would answer affirmatively. Then why aren't you a multimillionaire?

I would like to propose that people don't generally go to McDonald's for great food. They go there because *they get what they expect*, day in and day out. Let me explain it like this: Let's look at burgers on a scale between 1 and 10, with 10 being the best. If you create an expectation that you are going to deliver a level 10 burger, but you only produce a level 7 burger, you will be in trouble; whereas McDonald's can promise only a level 5 burger, but since they deliver a level 5 burger every day of the year, every hour of the day, in every country around the world, they are going to get the lion's share of the business.

"Why?" you ask. Because business is built on trust, not burgers. Trust means that you create expectations that you fulfill consistently. The fastest way to break trust is to overpromise and underperform. Remember this: Your *repetition* becomes your *reputation*. Advertising and marketing can get people in the door, but only consistency will keep them coming back.

Some businesses are bottom-feeders, barely surviving on some selfish, self-serving plot. I experienced shopping in one of these businesses recently. It was a jewelry store, and over the counter of the store hung a sign that read, *All sales are final. NO RETURNS accepted.* What a stupid way to do business! They were basically letting you know that once they got your money, you were screwed. If your wife does not like the ring you surprised her with from that store, you are stuck with it forever anyway. These businesses are one-hit wonders, based on profit from a single sale. Meeting your expectations is the least of their concerns, but great businesses thrive on fulfilled expectations.

The same can be said for your personal life. Many people are extremely gifted and are capable of delivering a level 10 every time they are up to bat (metaphorically speaking), but they are inconsistent, irresponsible and immature. Because they are so much more capable than the rest of the team members, they are often surprised that nobody wants them on their team. Yet you cannot count on them to perform consistently, because they lack character.

A culture of prosperity is rooted in trust that is built on consistency. Whether you are building a great company or just doing life with your friends, fulfilling the expectations you create is the pathway to a prosperous life.

The Law of Favor

Jesus said, "Make friends for yourselves by means of the wealth of unrighteousness, so that when it fails, they will receive you into the eternal dwellings" (Luke 16:9). This is such a radical concept coming from Jesus, because He just told us to make friends with money! Now, we all know that Jesus is not talking about bribing people or anything sinister like that. He simply is teaching us about the power of generosity. We certainly cannot transform cities if nobody likes us or if we have no favor with influencers. It is also true that there are many different ways to gain favor, but in a world influenced by Mammon, generosity really gets people's attention.

I have a crazy personal story that helped drive this point home for me. I have played basketball at the same YMCA twice a week for seventeen years. I am not a very good player, but I love the game, and it is great exercise. About eight years ago, the atmosphere in the gym changed from a bunch of guys playing a friendly game of basketball, to a competition with NBA-like intensity. My lack of talent made me the target of tons of animosity, as none of the good players wanted me to play there anymore, and they worked hard to make that clear. Soon they were bullying me, making fun of me and threatening me. This went on for four long years! I would come home so discouraged and often weeping, trying to understand how these young men could be so heartless.

Kathy would say, "You need to quit going to that gym. Take up golf, like most men your age! Those guys are going to hurt you." (I had been thrown to the ground twice on purpose that year).

I would argue, "I love basketball. I hate golf . . . and not only that, but I love the guys I play with. They just don't like me."

Then one day, after an exceptionally hard day at the gym, I was driving home in tears and the Lord said to me, *Why don't you make friends by using unrighteous Mammon?*

What's that? I inquired.

Money! He responded.

How do I do that? I questioned.

Think about it. You'll figure it out, was the divine response.

On the drive home, I asked myself who it was that everyone in the gym respected. Immediately, two men came to mind. They were the best players on the court, and all the men respected them a lot. Coincidentally, both men had obvious financial issues. I had observed them at the front counter on a regular basis, trying to negotiate the cost of their membership.

That day, I devised my scheme. I set it in motion the following Friday. I paid for both their annual memberships without telling either one of them. I had another tough day at the gym that week. But the following Monday, I walked into the gym and both men greeted me separately and thanked me for paying for their membership. What happened next was epic! When the game was about to begin, the guys started arguing over who *got* to have me on their team! The rest of the day was like a dream. I suddenly had favor with the two most respected men in the gym, and they both made sure that everyone knew it. Many years have passed since that day, and one of those two guys has moved away. But most everyone still loves me at the gym in spite of my lack of skill, and most don't even know why.

The Law of the Neighborhood

You have probably heard this law a hundred times, but the ramifications might be deeper than you think. Never buy the best house in the worst neighborhood, because you will relegate the power to influence the value of your investment to your neighbors. There will be no way you can improve the value of your house, because it is already the best house in the neighborhood. The only way your investment is going to grow in value is if the neighborhood improves dramatically, or some other outside condition changes. Buying the worst house in a great neighborhood is often the best investment you can make in any city.

Let's apply this principle to some other areas of life. Do you want to be the best player on a really bad team? Wouldn't it be better to be the least accomplished player on a really great team? Sometimes in our need to stand out, we find ourselves making really dumb decisions about life. In our ignorance we become kings of sand castles or neighborhood slumlords, instead of royal priests and children of God.

Remember, your life is one piece of a much bigger ecosystem. Be cognizant of your surroundings and how other people's ecosystems will affect your life.

The "Cut Bait and Run" Law

There is a tendency for us to pour more money into something than it will ever be worth. Often, this happens because we invest money into something like a car to fix it, but then it breaks again, so we pour even more money into it. At some point, the money we spent to fix it already *becomes the reason* why we are throwing more money at it.

Most of the time, we keep investing in something like that so we don't lose the money we already dumped into it. Yet it might just be time to sell the beast for whatever you can, and get out. Cut bait and run!

I have watched this cycle happen so often in the automotive repair business. People would bring their high-mileage car in for some major repair like a new engine, and I would try to explain to them that with the amount of miles on their vehicle, it really would not be wise to pour money into the engine. But they would do it anyway, and inevitably, a few months later the transmission would go out. By then, of course, they had so much money invested in the engine that what they had already spent became their rationale for rebuilding the transmission.

The Law of Margin

Many years ago I owned a consulting company called Cornerstone Consulting, which was dedicated to helping business people become more profitable (or in some cases profitable in the first place). It was astonishing to me how many business people actually did not understand the simplest concepts about money. Here is one important lesson that I call the Law of Margin. Let's say you pay $1 for a product and you sell it for $2. You just made $1 profit, or a 100 percent markup. Now let's suppose that you want to increase your sales, so you give your customer a 25 percent discount on the price, selling the product for $1.50. Your product cost (COG, or cost of goods) remained the same; consequently, your profit dropped by 50 percent, to 50 cents rather than $1.

In effect, you dropped your price 25 percent, but you reduced your profit by 50 percent. This means you now have to sell twice as much product just to break even. Lowering your prices without reducing your cost of goods (COG) is often the fastest way to go out of business.

On the other hand, if you raise the original price of your product just 10 percent, to $2.20, you will make 20 cents more, increasing your profits from $1 to $1.20, which is a 20 percent increase in profits. It is very important to keep an eye on how your COG is related to the price you are charging for your product, and how the price you set—or the sale you run—affects your profit margin.

If you want to establish a "sense" with customers that a product or service is worth a certain price no matter what the COG, then you can set the price and give a one-time discount to get into the market. For instance, if your COG on a product is $1 and you offer your product/service at $5.00, but then you give a one-time 50 percent discount, you just told your customer that the value of your product/service is $5, even though they are buying it at the hot-deal price of $2.50 initially. This worth is not based on the COG, but on some other criteria—for example, that your product saves the customers an hour a day on some task they perform. You just created another rationale for buying your product/service, based on what their time is worth to them. Wealth multiplies when the value of your product is not tied to the COG, but of course this only works if you have a corner on the market.

As an example of working with the law of margin, when I came to Bethel Church we were in trouble financially. We could not even meet our weekly payrolls. I started digging around to understand why a church with a thousand people in attendance could be so broke. At the time, Bethel Church hosted about four conferences a year. One of the first things I discovered was that all these conferences lost huge amounts of money. I started inquiring why the people who came to the conferences and benefited from the experience would not pay enough admission even to cover the cost of event.

"Well," one of our staff said, "when we raised the admission price to cover our costs, some people complained."

I was surprised by the answer. "Don't drop the price," I argued. "Improve their experience! And remember, even if you gave the conference away for free, some people would still complain."

The next conference we did, we raised our price to cover our costs and did our best to improve the conference attendees' experience. The truth is, in the past we had reacted to all complaints by just lowering the price, so we had never put any tools in place to measure the experience of our attendees. This time, we immediately enacted a conference survey to get feedback about their experience. The results were amazing. Our conferences improved dramatically, they were filled to capacity, and of course a few people still complained. Pricing is an art that needs to be taken seriously. The average business in America lasts fewer than two years. Much of this attrition can be attributed to a lack of understanding of the power of wealth. Many entrepreneurs understand their business, but they don't understand *business*. I have discovered that even people with MBAs, who may understand the complexities of the stock market, often don't know the ABCs of the creation of wealth.

The Law of the Triune Choice

We were in the auto parts business in the 1980s and '90s, as I mentioned before, and we grew to three stores in ten years. One of the first things I learned in that season was how to choose my business strategy by looking at the three basic elements of business: *price*, *quality* and *service*. I found that in order to be successful in business, it was necessary to choose any *two* of these three choices.

In other words, I could offer the lowest prices and the best service, but if I also wanted to offer the best-quality products, I eventually would not be able to compete. Or I could choose to offer the best service and the best products, but also trying to offer the cheapest price is a slow journey to the business boneyard. And of course, I could choose the lowest price and the highest-quality products, *but not all three at once!*

Think about it like this: Let's say you and I are competitors who offer basically the same products, and you choose to be the cheapest in price, with the best service and the highest-quality products. If I come along and offer a cheaper price and the best products, but not great service, my cost of doing business is less than yours. My cost of providing the product to the market is less. If you tried to match me, I could drop my price even lower. Soon your business model would become unsustainable.

Amazon and eBay are great case studies in the law of triune choices. They have chosen to offer the cheapest price, the best products and excellent service—in a way—but they ditched the brick-and-mortar store model so as to lower their cost of doing business dramatically. They have redefined what service is in their industry. For example, if I go to Best Buy, someone greets me at the door and helps me make the right product choice. The sales associate may give me technical advice and even help me with a simple installation, whereas there is no one to talk to at Amazon or eBay. Yet Amazon and eBay have excellent product rating systems and a customer advice section, so you can get a really good idea of what level of quality the products are, and you can find important facts about their use. There is also a much larger selection, as long as you don't mind waiting a day or three for your product. As of this writing, companies like Best Buy have gone to guaranteed price matching, which means they can be a little higher on some things and then cut the price to match online offers for anyone who cares. Amazon, on their part, has decided to open some brick-and-mortar stores, which I simply cannot understand. I guess time will tell if the law of triune choices will prevail in the world of technology.

The Law of Diminishing Investment

Simply stated, the law of diminishing investment means that you typically can fund the highest percentage of your ultimate goal with a relatively small percentage of your investment. It will require a relatively high percentage of your investment, however, to fund the final portion of your ultimate goal.

Let me illustrate: Let's say that a 60 percent investment in your endeavor gets you to 90 percent of your ultimate goal. This means it will cost you another 40 percent to fulfill the last 10 percent of your endeavor. If you are making high-end, one-of-a-kind watches for extremely rich people, then the choice is simple to go for 100 percent quality, because your clientele is willing to pay whatever the cost for the "perfect" watch.

But most of us are not in the high-end watch business, so you must ask yourself, at what point is your investment good enough for the purpose you have in mind? Who is your market, and what do they demand? Who is your competition, and where do they draw the line?

This principle is often at work in our personal lives. For example, is the $28,000 pickup truck with 90 percent of everything you want good enough? Or is it worth it to pay another $20,000 for a truck with all the bells and whistles . . . the truck of your dreams? The dealer wants to sell you the $48,000 truck with everything you want, plus a bunch of stuff you have never even heard of, because the dealer makes a lot more money on better-equipped vehicles. Dealers often make the sale by convincing you that your "dream truck" is available for the same *monthly payment* as your 90 percent satisfactory truck. Of course, you may lose sight of the fact that you will be making that "same" payment *forever*!

The Law of Risk

Solomon was the wealthiest king ever to live. He had so much gold that silver actually became worthless to him. When a guy like that has advice about investments, it is probably worth paying attention to him. So here is Solomon's wisdom on risk investment:

Cast your bread on the surface of the waters, for you will find it after many days. Divide your portion to seven, or even to eight, for you do not know what misfortune may occur on the earth. If the clouds are full, they pour out rain upon the earth; and whether a tree falls toward the south or toward the north, wherever the tree falls, there it lies. He who watches the wind will not sow and he who looks at the clouds will not reap. Just as you do not know the path of the wind and how bones are formed in the womb of the pregnant woman, so you do not know the activity of God who makes all things.

Ecclesiastes 11:1–5

Here are five takeaways from Solomon's wisdom on investments:

1. Cast your bread on the water, and it will come back to you sometime in the future.

    Point: *Make long-term investments that will pay dividends in the future. Poor people live for today, middle-class people live for their retirement, but wealthy people live to leave a legacy. Think legacy!*

2. Cast your portions to seven or eight because of misfortune.

    Point: *Spread your money out into several different types of investments to protect your assets from calamities that you cannot foresee.*

3. Clouds pour rain when they are full.

    Point: *An investment will come to maturity in due time, so be patient.*

4. A tree falls to the north or south; wherever it falls, it lies there.

    Point: *Don't gamble on which way the tree is going to fall. Rather, invest in the inevitable: The tree is going to fall. Financing a future sure thing is not gambling, whereas wagering your hard-earned money on elements that are unpredictable is probably not prudent.*

5. He who watches the wind and rain will not sow, and he who watches the clouds won't reap. You don't know how bones form in a pregnant woman, nor do you understand the activities of God.

   Point: If you wait for the perfect conditions to do business, you will never invest. But if you entrust your investments to God, He will make them flourish in mysterious and sometimes miraculous ways.

This chapter obviously is not the final word on creating wealth. Rather, it is meant to get you thinking practically about your own prosperity journey. If you have a lot of business experience, this chapter may have seemed too elementary. But if that is not you, perhaps this is the beginning of a new way of thinking.

Wherever you are in life, I want to challenge you to cultivate a proactive plan for your future. You should consider developing at least five streams of income (Kathy and I have twelve) so that you are not relying on your "job" as the only—or even primary—source of revenue. And finally, invest in your grandchildren's future. In fact, dream of a generation you will never see, and sow into their lives. Solomon put it this way: "A good man leaves an inheritance to his children's children" (Proverbs 13:22). This is the path of the noble, the way of the wealthy!

11

Mastering Motivation

Having a wealth plan in place is important. Investing in the future is a sign of your nobility, but you cannot make the journey alone; you will need a team of people who can help you fulfill your God-given plan. In fact, if your plan does not require others to co-labor with you, then you don't have God's plan for your life. God's plan is always bigger than you. Yet the truth is that getting people on your bus and figuring out how to motivate them toward a noble goal is one of the most exhilarating and frustrating things you can do in life.

The Spirit of '76

Our first real attempt at building a team that would actually accomplish something together was in 1980, when Kathy and I purchased our first business. Nestled in the Trinity Alps of Northern California, it was an old Union 76 Station, with a huge orange 76 ball that glowed at night and turned 360 degrees. We called our business Cornerstone

Union 76, and we were determined to impact the universe with our world-class service.

Our first challenge was finding qualified employees, especially automotive technicians, who had a good attitude and work ethic in a town of three thousand people. This proved to be a near-miraculous adventure. Then getting them to work together at some level of harmony and at a pace that made the business at least marginally profitable required extraordinary miracles. Furthermore, winning enough local customers to keep this team of miracle workers funded in the dead of winter, with three feet of snow on the ground and 28 degrees on the thermometer, well, you get the idea . . . it was beyond challenging.

This was the era of full-service gas stations, which required island salesmen (or as we affectionately called them, *Petroleum Transfer Engineers*) to serve the customers at the pump island. In those days, cars actually broke down. In fact, you had to get your vehicle's engine tuned up every 12,000 miles. Your car required you to add oil to it between oil changes, and you rarely got more than 30,000 miles on anything rubber, as in fan belts and radiator hoses. If you tried to beat the system, your car typically came in on a tow truck. So one of the important tasks that an island salesman performed (besides filling up your tank) was checking under the hood, checking your tire pressures, and washing all your windows.

Getting gas in those days was kind of an event, and because you wanted to make sure someone pointed out potential problems with your vehicle before the dreaded tow hook came to drag it to the shop, you typically built a trust relationship with your local service station. Furthermore, the service station dealer made only two to five cents a gallon off gasoline, so it often cost more to sell it than he made on the product. Those smart oil companies convinced us that gasoline was a "loss leader," and that we should make our profit off the repairs and service of the vehicles that came in for fuel.

The pump island salesmen were therefore an integral part of making a service station profitable, since it was their job to "sell" needed parts and service to our customers. (Sell, in this case, meant pointing out the vehicle's needs to the customer. Every customer feared the tow hook, so sales were not brain surgery.) Unfortunately, this task was most often relegated to minimum-wage high school kids on the evening shift and young guys clueless about life on the day shift . . . I mean, the job was not exactly a career opportunity.

I know what you are thinking: *Kris, why are you recounting the history of the ancient world in a book on wealth?*

Good question. It is because I am trying to help you understand the significance of what we accomplished with the Lord's insights, against truly incredible odds. I want you to understand that with His insights, you, too, can accomplish amazing things against all odds.

Island Fever

When we took over the station, my first task was to teach my four young salesmen, who literally had never worked a day in their lives before this job, how to provide great service and sell needed products to my precious customers. I devised a generous commission plan in which they were paid $5 per tire, $2 per fan belt, 50 cents per quart of oil, $2 per air filter and $5 for every oil change they sold. The first day, I had them all watch me wait on all the customers myself for 8 hours while they asked questions. That day I sold 12 tires, 15 fan belts, 5 oil changes, and numerous air filters and quarts of oil. The next day they waited on the customers, while I watched and trained them. By the second week they had the job down really well, so I let them go it alone, with me nearby.

That first month, these guys sold nothing but a few cans of oil in thirty days! So I repeated the training, complete with a motivational speech. Again the next month, they sold *nothing*.

One day it finally became clear to me that this was not a training issue; this was lack of motivation on their part. I let them have it that day! When I got home that night, I was angry with my young team. I decided to go talk to the Lord about the situation, at Kathy's request.

Lord, I moaned, *I have this problem. I'm trying to motivate my young team, but nothing I do seems to work.*

Meet them in the season of life they are in and motivate them from there, He responded.

What season is that? I inquired.

Instant gratification, the Lord said.

I spent the evening thinking about how to motivate young men who had an instant gratification mindset. Their commission check was being paid to them once a month, so I gathered my team and explained that from now on, we would pay them their commission every Friday. They seemed excited at our change in policy, and I anticipated a large increase in sales.

Another week passed, and by the next Friday I realized that nothing had changed. My young team had managed to sell ten quarts of oil and nothing else. I was beginning to lose heart. I went back to the Lord and inquired again. He reminded me that He had said *instant gratification*.

The next Monday, I gathered my island salesmen and informed them that I would pay them their commission every day after each of their shifts. They seemed really pleased about the new policy. Of course, the administration of a daily commission was a nightmare. But that week, my grateful band of future salesmen of America sold no product—not a thing.

I wanted to scream. "What's wrong with you guys?" I scolded. "What's it going to take to get you guys to do your jobs?"

To which they replied, "Don't know . . . not sure . . . sorry, Boss! Bad on us, Boss man!"

I went back to the Lord and let Him know in no uncertain terms that He was wrong about my band of knuckleheads. *I've taken Your counsel and listened to Your wisdom, but nothing works! I've been Your servant, and You haven't—*

Kris! the Lord interrupted, *I said I-N-S-T-A-N-T gratification! You, My son, didn't pay attention!*

Yikes! Monday, I gathered my band of brothers and let them know that when they sold any product, they could put the sales receipt in the drawer and immediately take their commission out of the cashbox. They hooted like a bunch of cowboys on a cattle drive. I knew then that I was on to something. The first month, they sold so many products and services that I had to hire two more mechanics just to keep up with the increased demand. Soon we had so much business that our customers' cars lined both sides of the street for half a mile. Before the year was over, we had to rent the yard across the street from the station to park more cars. By the end of our second year of business, we opened another shop called Cornerstone Fleet Repair to try to keep up with all the business my young band of supersalesmen sold. The following year, we launched a third shop called Foreign Affairs as our business grew exponentially.

My friend and competitor, Larry, from the Chevron station across the street, came over one day and asked if we could talk.

"Sure, what's up?" I replied.

"What's your secret, man? I mean, how are you attracting all this business in this little town?" he begged.

"I pay my island guys commission," I revealed.

"I do, too," he shot back in defense. "How much do you pay?"

I showed him the commission charts, which he studied like a dog with a new bone.

Finally, with a bewildered look on his face, he replied, "My commission program is nearly identical!"

"Well, I guess my young men are just more motivated, Larry," I said. I never did tell him my secret formula, but by our fifth year we were feeding Larry the overflow from our three shops and keeping him pretty busy.

More Troubles

We grew to employ seven technicians, one serviceman, two parts men, and a service writer. We took care of every single fleet account in the entire county—PG&E, Sierra Pacific, Continental Telephone, Trinity Sheriff, Trinity Probation, Highway Patrol, U.S. Forest Service, Caltrans, Trinity Ambulance, Tops Market—yet we were losing money like water! In June 1984, I walked into my accountant's office and sat down. He leaned over his big oak desk and said, "Kris, you're bankrupt, and you're the only one who doesn't know it!"

I hired a consultant to help me understand what was wrong. Two months later, he laid out the ugly truth on the shop floor in front of me. In an average 40-hour workweek, my technicians charged only 10 hours to the customers. Do the math: If we paid the technicians $15 per hour and our shop rate was $40 per hour, but it took them *four* man hours to be able to charge out *one* shop hour, then it cost Cornerstone $60 to make $40. In other words, the more work we did, the more money we lost!

It was clear what we had to do to save our sinking ship. We had to find a way to motivate our technicians to become much more efficient. We devised a plan to bonus them at various levels of efficiency each month: $100 for 50 percent efficiency, $200 for 60 percent, $300 for 70 percent, $400 for 80 percent, $500 for 90 percent, $600 for 100 percent, per their charged hours. (In other words, If Johnny worked 100 hours in a month and was able to charge out 60 hours to the customers, he received a $200 bonus, and so on). After all my hoopla and hype was done, only one of our seven technicians actually improved his productivity. I was pretty frustrated. Then when I was driving home one day from work, I saw all our men playing softball on a team in the summer heat. I thought to myself, *Why will our men run around the bases for free in a softball game, but they won't rush to finish a brake job for money?*

Suddenly I heard the Lord whisper, *When you find the answer to that question, you'll begin to prosper!*

I pondered that question for days, and then I heard this word from the Lord: *The power of competition.*

Okay, how can we turn our problem into their game? I thought. Suddenly I got an idea. I had Kathy take our seven technicians' productivity and build a bar chart for *labor charged* versus *hours worked daily and monthly* totals. The chart compared each day and month's production efficiency against each technician. Then I took the chart and posted it on the wall for all our employees to see. I updated the chart every day.

When the guys walked in that first morning and saw the chart on the wall, they had very different responses. The technician who was leading in efficiency predictively had my favorite response: "Hey guys, I'm kicking your butts!"

To which the others responded with comments of their own: "Hey, my productivity is no one else's business. . . ." "Yeah! I agree. . . ." "Well, if I got all the gravy jobs like Mike, I would be blowing all you guys away. . . ." "Shut up, man. You're so full of yourself!"

They argued all day, mostly trying to excuse their poor performances. The guy with the worst stats quit a week after I posted the charts. That is when I knew my plan was working perfectly. Soon I was hearing a bunch of passionate feedback about our shop equipment, facilities and tools. The comments went something like this: "Boss, if you want me to be productive, you need to buy another rack. I spend half the day waiting for a lift!"

The funny thing is, these guys had never complained once in three years about our equipment or tools. Now they were making me lists of stuff they needed every week. I began investing in their lists every day, and their productivity grew by over 300 percent.

Another serious problem soon emerged. Team members who used to get along so well became so competitive that they refused to help each other. I thought, *Lord, I've created a monster to make money!*

Then one day the Lord gave me the passage out of Romans where it says that we are "individually members one of another" (Romans 12:5). Somehow, I had to figure out how to develop a reward system that inspired competition *and* camaraderie. I got another idea; I gathered my guys and added another level of bonus to their commission. This time, I told them I would give them each a $200 bonus every month that every single technician was above 70 percent efficiency. But if one person was even 1 percent below the minimum efficiency required, everyone would lose the bonus. (Three of our techs were commonly under the 70 percent minimum, primarily because the rest of the team members were so unhelpful and selfish.)

At first, their response was less than noble as the efficiency leaders began threatening the rest of the technicians. Of course, the other techs defended themselves and the whole thing got pretty ugly. But these guys were buddies who played softball together and hung out as families, so I figured they would work it out. By the second week, the best techs were helping the less experienced guys and teaching them faster ways to accomplish their tasks. Soon the entire team was working together in harmony, and consequently they earned their team bonus nearly every month. But the most exciting thing to me was that Cornerstone was suddenly "born again." Our labor sales grew by 300 to 400 percent in just six months—but the best news is that sales continued to increase every year after that.

When you increase revenue without increasing expenses, the result is a huge growth in profit. By the sixth year, we launched our first auto parts store called Crossroad Auto Parts. We took the principles we learned from that tiny Union 76 station and used them to grow our parts business into three locations in ten years.

Maybe you just spent the last several minutes reading this chapter and thinking, *I'm never going into business, so I'm not sure what to do with these business principles. . . .*

Actually, these are not "business principles." These are principles for life that I have demonstrated in a business narrative. This is the same way Jesus demonstrated truth. He told stories about farming, making money, and virgins with lamps, all for a broader audience than the analogy itself. For example, whether or not you are a farmer, you still need to understand the parable of the sower and the seed, or the wheat and the tares, because Jesus did not share these parables to make you a great farmer. He taught them to grow you as a son or daughter of God.

Reward Is Spiritual

What can we learn from the service bays of the Union 76 station? First, we must understand that the Kingdom of God is rooted in a culture of reward. The author of the book of Hebrews said it best: "Without faith it is impossible to please Him, for he who comes to God must believe that He is and that He is a *rewarder* of those who seek Him" (Hebrews 11:6, emphasis added). The apostle Paul echoed this sentiment when he wrote to the Corinthians, "Now he who plants and he who waters are one; but each will receive his own *reward* according to his own labor" (1 Corinthians 3:8, emphasis added). Of course, no commentary on reward would be complete without hearing from Jesus Himself, who said, "Behold I am coming quickly, and My *reward* is with Me, to render to every man according to what he has done" (Revelation 22:12, emphasis added).

Some people think they are being spiritual by not doing things in order to get stuff, but the truth is, you were created to long for reward. It is in your DNA, and it is part of your divine nature. The Bible says that "for the joy set before Him" Jesus endured the cross (Hebrews 12:2). Jesus died for the sake of reward.

How you manage your appetite for reward is vital to who you are becoming. Whether you will be a noble person or scoundrel is up to you. But denying that you want a reward is not humility; it is stupidity! So get over yourself, watch your motives, and use reward to inspire and provoke you to accomplish great things for the Kingdom.

Wise Leadership

Leading people in accomplishing tasks is an art that is actually rooted in understanding what kind of rewards motivate people in different seasons of their lives. Let me identify three simple seasons that are common to everyone, and then I will unpack what people's passions are that align with those seasons. The most basic motivation in life is *survival*. I work to feed, clothe and shelter myself and those within my care. The next essential passion in all of us is the desire for *connection*. We all want to be known and cared about. And once we are convinced and reassured that somebody loves us (preferably several people), then we begin to long for *significance*. We want to feel as though our life matters.

A wise leader discerns the seasons of people's lives and uses that information to inspire and influence his or her team. Let me share a short story with you to demonstrate how this works. A young man named Henry worked for me as a technician at the Union 76 station. Henry had a wife and two young kids and had been out of work for a couple of years. Consequently, he was barely able to feed his family or keep a roof over their heads. So Henry was highly motivated by money; he worked all the overtime he could get. He also performed well for raises and bonuses, so anytime I needed Henry to learn a new skill or master a different type of car, I just offered to give him a bonus when he was proficient at my goal.

Things were great between us, and Henry became our very best technician because he was so hungry. But about the fifth year of Henry's employment, something dramatic shifted in him that took me over a year to figure out. He stopped wanting to work overtime, he often refused to learn a new skill, and money ceased to motivate him. I tried everything I could think of to inspire him, including raises and bonuses, but nothing worked. Finally I came to realize something: When people achieve the ability to live at the economic level outside themselves that they are living inside themselves, they have just exited the land of mere existence.

In other words, everyone has a dream of what the perfect life looks like in his or her heart. For example, maybe it is the little house on the hill, with the white picket fence around it. When they obtain the financial ability to apprehend that house, money is no longer a motivator in their lives. It will take a new strategy to inspire these people.

It is important to understand that the need for approval and the need for significance are not the same thing. The need for approval makes a person want to fit in, and it is driven by the desire to feel connected. This drive for approval is part of the *connection* season. But the need for *significance* makes people want to stand out. Significance and connection are two different epoch seasons in life that sometimes collide simultaneously in the soul of a man. Henry was in a crisis of his soul, stuck between significance (wanting to stand out) and connection (needing approval). But something powerful was about to change.

Our entire team respected Henry, so he sort of journeyed through the land of *connection* at the same time he was leaving the land of *survival*. But the day we posted the efficiency charts on the wall, a new era was born in Henry's life. Henry's need for *significance* was suddenly met when he was recognized as the most productive employee, the star of the Cornerstone team. It touched something so deep in his soul that he began to work the way Michael Jordan played basketball in championship games. The man was a house on fire! Not only was he making me tons of money; he was happy again . . . alive . . . funny and inspiring. Although the rest of the team was in *survival* or *connection* mode at the time, they fed off Henry's enthusiasm, which caused our shop to become electric with passion.

Sometimes entire organizations have a "Henry moment" as the members of a team simultaneously awaken to a level of significance previously unattainable to them. This dynamic often occurs when fame and/or fortune are introduced abruptly into a culture. Leading people who are in survival or connection mode, and who are watching somebody else on the team suddenly move into a place of significance (fame or fortune), can be heart-wrenching. The way we manage this cultural transition determines whether or not these opportunities become constructive or destructive.

Soul Power

One of the ramifications of not understanding the dynamics of the soul is that you tend to rule your environment with fear, shame or manipulation. These tools may provide you with short-term wins, but they have long-term negative side effects. Living in an environment that is inwardly hostile toward you for punishing your team into performing is not just unwise; it is dumb. Don't be a lazy leader; be as wise as a serpent and as innocent as a dove (see Matthew 10:16). Use tools that have positive effects. Let's expand on our motivational tools:

1. You always get what you reward. First, decide what it is you want your team actually to accomplish. Next, figure out what the reward looks like and how that reward is going to be tied directly to the goal.

   • Giving a team member a bonus that is not tied to performance goals might help the person be loyal, but probably not productive.

   • Providing the reward even though the team member falls short of the goal undermines the purpose of goal setting.

   • If you set goals so high that nobody can obtain them without a miracle, you defeat the reason for goal setting, which is creating urgency.

2. The reward must be viable to be valuable. Let me explain it with a modified example of my story above. Let's say that instead of rewarding the technicians with $200 for 60 percent efficiency, you reward them with $10,000. You just created an unsustainable reward system, because the reward is more money than the business earned through the extra production. Now let's view it a different way. What would happen if you gave the team $2 for 60 percent efficiency? Probably not much! The reward is just not congruent with the task.

3. The reward system must be progressively constant to be properly motivating. For example, if you pay $500 for 60 percent efficiency but you only pay $100 for 80 percent efficiency, your system actually rewards more for doing less and less for doing more.

177

Although this example makes the principle obvious, leaders ignorantly do this very thing all the time in less apparent ways.

4. If you fail to deliver the reward you promised in a timely manner, then you might as well throw out the entire system. It is better not to promise something than to promise and not perform.

5. Changing the goal or reward in the middle of the season, or worse yet, in the middle of the month, is devastating, dishonest and unfair. The reward system should have a clearly communicated duration, including start and finish dates.

6. The reward system must address the side effect of the reward itself. For example, if the techs are working faster to get the reward, but their work gets sloppy and results in many more warranty claims, then the reward system must also become the deterrent. For example, in our system, if a car came back for a warranty on the work Henry did and it was his fault, Henry lost the commission he received for that job, and he also lost that same amount of money against his current commission.

7. If the reward system does not take into account the season people are in (like my high school guys in instant gratification mode, or Henry's need for significance, not money), then the system will not work.

8. If the reward system fixes one problem (for instance, productivity), but breaks something else (like morale), then adjust the system to enhance them both.

9. Lots of things are more motivating than money, especially outside the business world, so if money is tight or unavailable,

then be creative about the way you reward people. Recognition is a great way to motivate people. Things like employee or teammate of the month are beautiful ways to inspire them. A reserved parking space displaying a note of recognition for a person's outstanding service is another way to inspire people. An email blast about the accomplishment of a team member is also a great morale builder.

Reward versus Recognition

I think this is a good time to clarify how different kinds of reward systems give rise to various types of outcomes. There is a big difference between a *reward* and *recognition*. A reward must have performance goals attached to it, but recognition is acknowledging a person's contribution to the organization. You will not motivate people to be more efficient by giving them random bonuses for being great employees. Bonus systems that are not tied to agreed-upon, clearly communicated target criteria will not *consistently* lead to productivity. Random bonuses say "thank you," and done right, they can really boost morale, which does enhance performance indirectly. But be careful—recognizing an employee who obviously is performing poorly will send the wrong message to the rest of the team and will probably backfire on you.

In life and at work, you will always have certain people you enjoy and like more than others. And you will sometimes have teammates you actually don't like, or at least don't enjoy. That is your prerogative as a person. But as a leader, your reward and bonus systems have to be just—not twisted to reward your friends or to punish those who don't have favor with you. In your personal life, you can give your friends gifts after hours all you want. But treating people in an organization or a workplace with favoritism, without performance qualifiers that others around them can also attain, will undermine your entire wealth culture.

The Art of Goal Setting

The purpose of a reward system is threefold:

#1   Create urgency in a culture and funnel it toward performance goals.

#2   Improve productivity by focusing effort and energy on recognized objectives.

#3   Create an atmosphere of fun through competition.

Let me give you an analogy to help you with the art of goal setting. Let's say you are supposed to catch a bus at 3:00 p.m. and you arrive sixty seconds late. As you walk up to the bus, the door closes and it starts to roll away. Are you going to run after the bus and try to get the driver to open the door? Most likely.

Now let's change the scenario. This time you arrive five minutes late and the bus is three blocks down the road. Are you going to chase the bus? No way! There is no chance you will ever catch that bus (barring a miracle).

Think of setting goals in terms of my bus analogy; you want the culture to have a sense of urgency. Urgency is your secret invisible master manager. You don't pay him, he never takes a vacation, and he is great to have in the lunchroom. But most importantly, he is managing the productivity of your team while you are away.

"That's great. How do I hire Mr. Urgency?" you inquire.

Good question! He only works for people who understand the art of goal setting. If you give someone 40 hours to do a 20-hour job, what hour will they finish it? Yep, you guessed it—in the fortieth hour. If you give someone a 20-hour job and give them 10 hours to finish it, will they rush to try to get it done? No! Because like the bus that is three blocks down the road when you arrive, there is no chance of catching that bus. There is no chance you will finish a 20-hour task in 10 hours.

How about if I give you 19 hours to complete a 20-hour task? Will you finish then? Yes! That is like the bus that rolls away just as you get to the bus stop. You will chase it. That is the world that Mr. Urgency works in, the world of realistic but ambitious goals.

To create a culture that employs Mr. Urgency, it is paramount that these three elements are present:

#1 Well-defined goals that everyone understands

#2 Timelines that are very well-thought-out and lean toward just enough time to accomplish the tasks agreed upon

#3 A feedback system in which everyone in the environment always knows the score, metaphorically speaking

In other words, there is a way for the people who have been tasked with a certain duty to know where the task falls in the time continuum of the ultimate goal. If we are painting the office by Friday, the task itself is a feedback system. Everyone can look at the wall and see what has been accomplished so far, and of course they know what day it is. But many tasks will need a more complex scoring system since it is not as easy to know if the task is on schedule. You cannot expect people to hit targets if the reporting is slow, inaccurate or not available for everyone to view.

World Changers

Like the stewards in the parables of the talents and the minas, the goal is to create wealth cultures in which money makes money. If we could learn how to create ecosystems of wealth, we could help people succeed in life without needing government subsidies. Learning how to motivate people is one of the secrets of a wealth culture. I want to inspire you to become more than a hard-working, faithful steward. Instead, become a world changer by inspiring people to follow you in doing something truly great for the Kingdom!

12

The Company You Keep

Somebody once said, "Show me a man's friends and I will tell you about that man's character." We should love everybody and never neglect the poor or needy, but the people whom we allow to influence us really determine our future.

Everywhere I go, people seem obsessed with finding their destiny. The million-dollar question appears to be, "Why am I alive, and what was I born to do?" I have taught people for years that next to finding God, the most important thing they can do in life is find their purpose. But I was wrong!

The truth is, you cannot find your purpose until you have found your people, because your ultimate purpose is in your people. People ask me all the time if I had a vision when I was a boy for the ministry I am in. No! My vision grew out of the role I play with the people I am called to be in community with. We are the Body of Christ. If I am a finger, I need to connect with a hand. If I am an eye, I need to find my place in the head, and so forth. I simply cannot find my ultimate destiny without finding my God-given place in the Body. (If you would like to know more about how and where to find your people, read my book *Destined to Win* [Thomas Nelson, 2017], in which I dedicate two chapters to this subject.)

With that being said, we should prayerfully and proactively choose whom we allow to influence us. When Moses came down from the mountain, he was glowing like a lightbulb. He had to put a veil over his face for the sake of the people. That veil filtered the way people perceived him and the way Moses saw the world. Our friends inspire so much of the way we view and translate the world around us. Solomon said it like this: "Leave the presence of a fool, or you will not discern words of knowledge" (Proverbs 14:7). He also said, "He who walks with wise men will be wise, but the companion of fools will suffer harm" (Proverbs 13:20). And the great apostle Paul always blows me away with his insights. (The guy is so blunt!) He writes, "Do not be deceived: 'Bad company corrupts good morals'" (1 Corinthians 15:33).

My point is that the company you keep matters a lot . . . a whole lot. Many people have friendships that are an inch deep and a mile wide. Proverbs 18:24 says, "A man of too many friends comes to ruin, but there is a friend who sticks closer than a brother." I am talking about real friends who stick closer than a brother—people you do life with, whom you respect and who respect you. They will mold your soul and anchor your core values into their "accent" (the way they see things) for life.

One of the dynamics I have observed on our Bethel Church teams is that often, they are negatively impacted by the mindset of the broken people they set out to help. A conversation I had a while back at lunch with a few of our outreach pastors characterizes my point. These pastors' primary ministry is to the homeless and extremely poor. One of them began to recount to me how sad it is that the middle-class people of our city don't want the homeless and poor in their neighborhoods and in front of their businesses.

"They aren't compassionate people who understand the plight of these broken people," this pastor scolded. The others chimed in with their amens.

I was noticeably silent until they finished their comments. Then I said, "Guys, the homeless live a life of selfishness and destruction. They don't work, and they make no positive contribution to our community. They steal from our business people, begging in front of their businesses and driving their hard-earned customers away. Many of them throw their garbage all over our streets and make a huge mess on our beautiful riverbanks. That's why middle-class people don't want them around. And by the way, the need for understanding should flow both ways. Being poor doesn't give you the right to be insensitive to the needs of others around you, including the business people you hurt."

The pastors looked at me as if I were speaking Martian or something. I went on to tell them, "You'll never give anyone a hand up by getting down in the mental mud with those who have a victim mentality."

Chucking stones at the provision palace will not help you lift the poor out of poverty. It will, however, succeed in building an "us and them" mentality. Personally, I have worked with the poor for four decades, and I am on a team commissioned to help solve the homelessness issue in our community. I am therefore aware that many of our homeless and extremely poor friends are mentally ill and/or really hurting. They need much more compassion than I expressed to my team above. But again, my point is that we cannot become like the people we help in order to understand their plight and see them truly freed from that bondage.

My Best Friend

The ultimate way to transform your thinking to a wealth mentality is to hang around people who think from a wealth perspective. There is no better place to start than with God Himself. But I am afraid that we are becoming overly familiar with the God we barely know. Knowing God from a distance, or studying Him as you would the life of Winston Churchill, or dissecting Him like a frog is nothing like having a real friendship with Him. In the book of John, Jesus taught us that God wants to prune us the way a vinedresser prunes a grapevine back to its place of fruitfulness. He went on to explain that we are pruned by allowing Jesus to speak correction to us and by embracing His discipline from the heart, which is how we are being pruned with a promise (see John 15:1–11).

Pruning begins the process of abiding in Christ, which in turn causes us to be friends with God—friends who are allowed to benefit from our relationship with Him. In fact, Jesus said, "If you abide in Me, and My words abide in you, ask whatever you wish, and it will be done for you" (John 15:7). In other words, if you let Jesus influence your heart, attitude and actions, He will let you influence Him and will give you anything you wish. Now *that* will destroy the poverty mentality in you! (This promise is so powerful! But as I said in chapter 2, it does not mean that based on selfish motives, we can name and claim anything we want. Let's not miss the fact that this privilege is only for those who meet the *abiding* requirements that we just talked about.)

Then Jesus went on to say, "No longer do I call you slaves, for the slave does not know what his master is doing; but I have called you friends, for all things that I have heard from My Father I have made known to you" (John 15:15). This is the ultimate climax of human interaction with God—a person bonding so closely with his or her Creator that they become intimate friends in a relationship in which they share their closest secrets.

This transition from slavery to friendship with God introduces us into a realm of revelation that only Jesus walked in, as I mentioned in chapter 7. I think of this level of supernatural revelation as *Google God*, except from the heart, not your head. What better way is there to move out of a poverty mindset and into a wealth mentality than to grow from a master/slave relationship into a friendship with God, who knows no impossibilities?

There is a startling fact here, held just below the surface of the waters of revelation, about the root cause of poverty: A slave does not know what his or her master is doing. So poverty is not a lack of money; it is a lack of revelation. The Old Testament story of Joseph gives us a great example of how withholding information enslaves people. Joseph interpreted Pharaoh's dreams as being about seven years of plenty, followed by seven years of famine. Then Joseph wisely instructed Pharaoh to store 20 percent of all the grain in Egypt during the seven years of abundance, so there would be enough food to feed the nation during the famine (see Genesis 41). But Joseph withheld the revelation about the coming famine and the plan to store food from the Egyptian population. The result was that all the Egyptian inhabitants became slaves as they sold themselves to Pharaoh for food. Here is the account:

> "Why should we die before your eyes, both we and our land? Buy us and our land for food, and we and our land will be slaves to Pharaoh. So give us seed, that we may live and not die, and that the land may not be desolate."
>
> So Joseph bought all the land of Egypt for Pharaoh, for every Egyptian sold his field, because the famine was severe upon them. Thus the land became Pharaoh's.
>
> Genesis 47:19–20

If Joseph simply had shared with the Egyptian people the same revelation that he gave to Pharaoh, the Egyptians would have become the richest people on the planet, because the famine affected the entire known world and people were coming from every nation to purchase food. Instead, Joseph's *secret*, the information he withheld, created a two-class system (rich and poor), and a first-world nation to become a third-world nation in one generation. The next pharaoh who rose to power enslaved the Israelites (see Exodus 1). Joseph enslaved the Egyptians, and the next generations of Egyptians enslaved the Israelites. In other words, what you sow, you will reap!

Now think about Africa, which is the poorest continent in the world by nearly every economic indicator, yet the richest continent in the world in natural resources. This fact alone makes it clear that Africa's problem is not money. I would like to propose that the poverty there is driven by a lack of revelation and understanding. Furthermore, if Joseph could turn a first-world country into a third-world country simply by withholding revelation about Pharaoh's dream, then it stands to reason that such a process could be reversed. Africa could transition from a third-world country to a first-world country simply by changing its status with God from slavery to friendship. In fact, the dream is already alive as many African believers who have become friends with God are changing the continent of Africa with their revelations and insights. It is just a matter of time before Africa will be one of the wealthiest continents in the world.

Changing Friends

In the last few years, I have found great favor with a few wealthy people and have discovered that "possibility thinking"—the idea that everything is possible—is very inspiring. The mindsets of these people awakened something so deeply asleep in me that I did not even know it was inside me. Just being in the same room with them, while dialoguing about the challenges in our city, is exciting and stimulating. They take everybody in the room to a new level of thinking. My friend Michael Clifford is one of the most amazing people I have ever met. He created two start-up companies in his garage that were taken public and made billions of dollars. For instance, he bought a near-bankrupt school called Grand Canyon University that was $40 million in debt and was losing $16 million per year. Then he assembled a team of leaders who transformed it into a world-class university making $400 million per year. The team he recruited took the university public with an Initial Public Offering (IPO), which at the time of this writing was valued at $4 billion. This was not a lucky fluke; it is a way of life for Michael and his business partners. This is what he does, and he does it day in and day out . . . all the time. Michael creates, as he has done with Jack Welch, Forbes and now Apple founder Steve "Woz" Wozniak, and he always swings for the fences. He says that he has had more failures than successes, but it is in failure that experience creates successes.

I have had a relationship with Michael for five years that has grown deeper every year. It all began when Michael read my book *Spirit Wars* and it brought him out of the darkest time in his life. A few months ago, I decided to expose my Bethel Church leadership team to him. These are women and men of God who believe in miracles and have done some really amazing things, with His help. In a city of 89,000 people, they have built the largest SEVIS (Student and Exchange Visitor Information System) approved vocational school in America, with 2,400 full-time students, including 953 international students from 65 nations, along with nationals from 47 states. They have also built a record label that five years ago did $300,000 in revenue, and then they grew it to $11.3 million dollars in business last year, not to mention that its artists won six Dove awards along the way. This is the same team who built a church of 9,000 in weekend attendance, which is 10 percent of our city's population.

I tell you all that just to let you know that these folks are not wimps. When the meeting with them began and the niceties were complete, I asked Michael to speak. Michael is not a motivational speaker or anything like that; he is a behind-the-scenes leader. But suddenly, you could hear a pin drop. My team just sat there in some sort of shock, listening to someone who thinks much bigger than we do.

It took several minutes after Michael had finished for anyone even to make a comment or ask a question. Then something happened. Several of them began to catch the wind of revelation. Drafting off Michael, they started ideating on a whole new level. It was beautiful listening to our team imagining together a world the way God intended—a world of possibility, faith and extraordinary miracles.

A month ago, Michael and a few of my team members were interacting over the poverty issue in our community. Redding has one of the worst economies in the nation for a city of our size. Michael began talking about shifting our economy by transforming the financial ecosystem of our city. His ability to see the big picture and understand how things like education are catalytic to our economy is astounding. In the meeting, he began mapping out a plan that would inspire a prosperous city. Soon everybody was chiming in with equally powerful ideas. I left the meeting thinking, *If I could transport all the people I've been assigned to influence into that two-hour meeting, I wouldn't have to write this book!* It was that mind-altering.

Relegated to Small Thinking

I have lain in bed at night wondering why people like Michael don't have a ton more influence in our cities. Why aren't these people being invited to lead our communities out of poverty and into prosperity? I don't really get it!

I began engaging my social networking audience a few months ago to try to understand from a broader perspective why such people are not invited into the leadership of our nations. (I do understand that some wealth-minded people find their way to the top of the leadership pile in a relatively few nations, but not to the level that seems reasonable.) I started by posting a few short comments on my Facebook page about the benefits of the way the wealthy think. *Oh man!* I unleashed a firestorm of criticism that made it feel as if something had crawled out of hell and slithered its way onto the pages of my network wall. Worse yet, about 70 percent of the people who follow me on Facebook describe themselves as Christians. Here is a sample of a few of their comments:

—Rich people make me sick! They oppress the poor and steal money from the masses, while they live in their glass mansions!

—I say screw the rich! They're destroying our country!

—The rich get richer, and the poor get poorer. Jesus warned us about those wealthy pigs!

I got nearly 450 comments on my first post, many of which were nothing less than vile. I was floored. Okay, now I understood why people with wealth are often isolated to the ice castles of our communities. I discovered a wealth-phobic snake pit that would rival the prejudice of any ethnic or religious group in the world. Let me address a few of these negative ideologies with some thoughts of my own.

First off, the idea that wealthy people are inherently selfish, or that by the nature of their prosperity they oppress the poor, is a lie. Yes, *many* rich people oppress the poor, but many more wealthy citizens take care of the poor, create jobs and spend billions of dollars every year funding various projects that improve the lives of those around them. Some of the most obvious examples are Bill and Melinda Gates, who are two of the wealthiest people alive today. They are investing billions of dollars in Africa to shift the poverty mindset of that continent. You may not like their approach to the problem, but it is their money and they should be able to spend it any way they want.

Ray and Joan Kroc, the founders of McDonald's, not only put tens of thousands of people to work in entry-level jobs; they also left most of their fortune to The Salvation Army. Joan was actually the visionary giver of the family, and she is the one who gave most of their wealth away. The list goes on and on. People with names like Rockefeller, Henry Ford, Warren Buffett and Paul Allen, just to name a few, not only collectively provided jobs for millions of people, but also spent or spend billions to take care of others. My guess is that there are many more generous billionaires than there are selfish ones.

Part of the challenge is that most wealthy people give in secret, or else they would have an endless line of leeches sucking the life out of their souls. But giving in secret is only popular in heaven. On earth if you are wealthy, you must publicize your endeavors or risk being lynched by the entitled. In fact, if you have a nice car and/or house, many people will judge you as selfish, without so much as a conversation about your generosity.

The people who post horrible things about the wealthy are often the same people who don't think twice about praying for God to pay off their bills, get them a job that pays more money or help them buy a house. These can be great prayers, but the people who pray them can set such a double standard that it makes me crazy. I grew up among the poor, and I can tell you that there are many times more selfish people among the poor than there are among the rich.

The truth is, many people become wealthy because they are generous, and many others stay poor because they are not. Jesus said, "Give, and it will be given to you . . . pressed down, shaken together, and running over" (Luke 6:38). But if you are generous and Jesus gives you so much that it is running out all over, you better hide it or you will be branded a prosperity teacher and relegated to the halls of heresy.

Be the Best for the World

No matter what you do in life, people will judge your motives, methods and means. It is inevitable. There is an old adage that says, "If you are successful, you will win some false friends and some true enemies; succeed anyway!"

People who make the greatest impact in life are typically criticized in their lifetime and enshrined in glory after they are dead.

What I am saying is that if you want to make history, you will have to step out of the crowd of comfort, convenience and cowardice and press in to God's wealth mentality. Cultivating the mind of Christ will put you in an elite class of people—not because you are any better than anyone else, but because you dared to leave the shore of small, fearful thinking to venture out into the sea of possibility. Thomas Aquinas put it like this: "If the highest aim of a captain were to preserve his ship, he would keep it in port forever." Kingdom wealth always requires risk!

It is important to remember the lessons about poverty, riches and Kingdom wealth that you have learned on our journey together, so that you can embrace your God-given identity and fulfill your divine purpose. You will recall that the greatest effect of true Kingdom wealth is the positive influence it has on others.

That being said, I want to challenge you to join me on this journey to make an impact on the world for good, by the God who knows no impossibilities. The voyage will be exciting . . . even treacherous at times, but the sacrifice that greatness will require cannot be compared to the glory of the exploits we will do as we carry out heaven's mission. *May it be on earth as it is in heaven.* So be it!

Notes

Chapter 5: The Legacy of Prosperity

1. Founders Online, "John Adams to Abigail Adams, 12 May 1780," *National Archives*, https://founders.archives.gov/documents/Adams/04-03-02-0258#AFC03d260n4 (spellings have been updated).

Chapter 7: The Mindset of the Wealthy

1. Bob Thiele and George David Weiss, "What a Wonderful World," performed by Louis Armstrong, © 1967 ABC Records.

2. Kris Vallotton, *Heavy Rain: How to Flood Your World with God's Transforming Power* (Minneapolis: Chosen Books, 2016), 247–48.

3. Ibid., 234–35.

Kris Vallotton is the author of several books and is a much-sought after international conference speaker. He has a passion to see people's lives transformed and see them equipped as catalysts for world transformation.

In 1998, Kris cofounded the Bethel School of Supernatural Ministry in Redding, California, which has grown to more than two thousand full-time students. Kris is the senior associate leader at Bethel Church and has been part of Bill Johnson's apostolic team for four decades.

Kris is also the founder of Moral Revolution, an organization dedicated to a worldwide sexual reformation.

Kris and his wife, Kathy, have been happily married since 1975. They have four children and eight grandchildren.

You can contact Kris, read his blog and/or find out more about him and his other ministry materials at www.krisvallotton.com. You can also follow Kris on Facebook (www.facebook.com/kvministries), Twitter (@kvministries) and Instagram (kvministries).

Other Books and Messages by Kris Vallotton

BOOKS

Fashioned to Reign

Heavy Rain

Moral Revolution

Outrageous Courage

School of the Prophets

Spirit Wars

The Supernatural Power of Forgiveness

Destined to Win

Developing a Supernatural Lifestyle

The Supernatural Ways of Royalty

Basic Training for the Supernatural Ways of Royalty

Basic Training for the Prophetic Ministry

MESSAGES

Casting Vision, Catching Hearts

Developing a Legacy

Is Your House Haunted?

Fighting for Your Place in History

For the Love of God

From Paupers to Princes

Fear Is Not Your Friend

From the Pool to the River

Mercy Triumphs over Judgment

Leadership for an Epoch Season 1, 2 & 3

The Tipping Point

Living from Eternity

These and many other titles are available at
www.krisvallotton.com

Great Ways to Connect with Kris:

 Like Kris' page on Facebook: Kris Vallotton

Follow Kris on Instagram: kvministries

Follow Kris on Twitter: kvministries

Subscribe to Kris' channel on YouTube: kvministries

Visit krisvallotton.com:

• Read Kris' blog: Raw, Real & Relevant

• Listen to Kris' podcasts

• Find Kris' latest travel itinerary

✉ Subscribe to Kris' mailing list to get exclusive offers, weekly updates, & free downloads

Visit your app store:

• Download the ⟨K⟩ KV Ministries App

Catch Kris on Bethel.TV

More Dynamic Teaching from Kris Vallotton!

Visit krisvallotton.com for more information and a full list of his books.

More from Kris Vallotton!

God's crowning creation in the Garden was Woman. Yet the state of our world belies her true beauty and purpose. In this eye-opening new book, Kris Vallotton reveals God's true plan and purpose for all women—both in the Church and throughout creation. As sons and daughters of the King, it's time for men and women to work together to restore God's original design for biblical partnership.

Fashioned to Reign

Sharing his deeply personal story of demonic bondage, torment and ultimate deliverance, Kris Vallotton turns the idea of spiritual warfare as we know it on its head. He reveals the diabolical lies and strategies of the enemy and arms you with a bold new battle plan. Now you can win the invisible battle against sin and the enemy. Victory is within your grasp. Will you take hold?

Spirit Wars

In these pages Kris and Jason Vallotton recount the gripping, unembellished true stories of one woman's Spirit-led exploits around the globe. Let Tracy Evans's life inspire you to radical obedience, faith adventures and a wild trust in God's power and purpose for your life. Your life will never be the same.

Outrageous Courage

Curriculum Kits from Kris Vallotton

These kits were created to be worked through in a community setting, so they are perfect for small groups or church classes. Each curriculum expands on the topics covered in the books they are based on, and includes everything you need to go deeper with God and with others. **Visit krisvallotton.com for more information.**

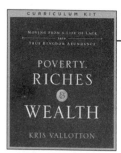

Poverty, Riches & Wealth

In this eye-opening study of what the Bible really says about poverty, riches and wealth, Kris Vallotton will shake up what you thought you knew, showing how you can experience true Kingdom wealth in every area of your life.

Spirit Wars

Kris Vallotton shares his personal story of demonic torment and ultimate deliverace. He reveals the lies and strategies of the devil and arms you with a new battle plan, so you can win the invisible battle against the enemy.

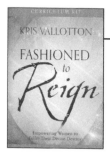

Fashioned to Reign

God's crowning creation in the Garden was Woman. Yet the state of our world belies her true beauty and purpose. In this book, Kris reveals God's true plan for all women—both in the Church and throughout creation.

Destined to Win

Destined to Win combines practical wisdom and profound revelation to unlock the latent potential present in each person. *Please note this study is available only as an e-course on Bethel.TV.*

The Supernatural Ways of Royalty

To experience the full inheritance that Jesus purchased at the cross, you must understand your royal identity. This study will help lead you into a powerful revelation of your supernatural inheritance.

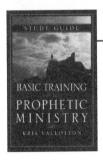

Basic Training for the Prophetic Ministry

The gift of prophecy is not reserved for a super-spiritual, elite group of Christians. If you are a Christian, the Holy Spirit lives inside of you. This means that you have access to all of His gifts and you too can prophesy!

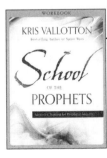

School of the Prophets

In this definitive guide, Kris Vallotton digs into one of the most crucial and controversial topics today: the office of the prophet. This study offers foundational teaching and provides critical advanced training.

Bethel School of Supernatural Ministry

bssm

We are committed to the truth that God loves people, gave Himself for them, and has given the Church supernatural power to bring individuals and nations into freedom. Our mission is to equip and deploy revivalists who whole-heartedly pursue worldwide transformation in their God-given spheres of influence. We are driven by a passion to raise up individuals who will go into all the world, say what He is saying, and do what He is doing.

We believe that with God, nothing is impossible.

FIND OUT MORE
bssm.net